I0393797

Financial Crimes Enforcement Network

Implications and Benefits of Cross-Border Funds Transmittal Reporting

January 2009

Executive Summary

Section 6302 of the Intelligence Reform and Terrorism Prevention Act of 2004 requires, among other things, that the Secretary of the Treasury study the feasibility of "requiring such financial institutions as the Secretary determines to be appropriate to report to the Financial Crimes Enforcement Network certain cross-border electronic transmittals of funds, if the Secretary determines that reporting of such transmittals is reasonably necessary to conduct the efforts of the Secretary against money laundering and terrorist financing."

Under current FinCEN regulation, 31 C.F.R. § 103.33 (the "recordkeeping rule")[1], financial institutions are generally required to collect and retain records of certain specified data regarding funds transfers they process of $3,000 or more. Because the recordkeeping rule does not distinguish between domestic and international funds transfers, financial institutions must make and maintain records on all transmittals of at least $3,000. Further, the rule states that while institutions need not retain the information in any particular manner, their records must be in a format that is retrievable. The recordkeeping rule does not require financial institutions to report to the Financial Crimes Enforcement Network (FinCEN) the information they maintain, but only requires that the data be available upon request to FinCEN, to law enforcement, and to regulators to whom FinCEN has delegated Bank Secrecy Act (BSA) compliance examination authority through the examination process.

In January 2007, FinCEN released a report on the Feasibility of a Cross-Border Electronic Funds Transfer Reporting System under the Bank Secrecy Act (BSA), hereafter referred to as "The Feasibility Study." The Feasibility Study concluded that the collection of Cross-Border Funds Transmittal (CBFT) data would be feasible. However, at the time, it was also determined that further analysis would be needed to assess the implications of CBFT reporting to the financial industry and the benefits to law enforcement.

In October 2007, FinCEN initiated a study to provide more details on the implications of CBFT reporting on the financial industry and the benefits to law enforcement. The results of that study, presented here, will be used to inform Treasury leadership's decision-making process in determining whether such reporting is reasonably necessary to conduct the efforts of the Secretary against money laundering and terrorist financing.

Scope and Approach

This study analyzed the implications of CBFT reporting on a portion of the U.S. financial services industry and the benefits to law enforcement of having access to CBFT data. The study team sought answers to the following questions:

- What technical solution would be required to support FinCEN's collection and use of CBFT data and what would be the costs to FinCEN of implementing this technology?
- If certain CBFT data were reported to FinCEN, what would be the known or potential uses of this information?

---

[1] See Section 31 C.F.R. § 103.33, Records to be made and maintained by financial institutions.

- What would be the effects on the affected U.S. financial services industry of a limited CBFT reporting requirement?
- How would the security and privacy of CBFT data be protected by FinCEN?

In order to answer these questions, the study team:

- Solicited input from the Bank Secrecy Act Advisory Group
- Surveyed the financial industry
- Interviewed financial institutions
- Interviewed law enforcement and regulatory agencies
- Interviewed foreign financial intelligence units that already collect CBFT data

Based on this input, the study team developed two potential operating models, documented the uses and usability of the data, developed a rough order of magnitude cost for each model, identified other potential implications for the financial industry, and documented how, going forward, to apply FinCEN's Information Technology (IT) security and privacy capabilities to CBFT data.

Potential Operating Models

In its earlier feasibility study, FinCEN concluded that the reporting responsibility should only apply to those U.S. financial institutions that exchange payment instructions directly with foreign institutions. FinCEN estimates this to include approximately 300 depository institutions and as many as 700 money transmitters with a very heavy concentration in the top few depository institutions and money transmitters. Both depository institutions and money transmitters are referred herein collectively as "financial institutions."

After analyzing the existing operating model, financial industry survey responses, and input gathered during financial institution and law enforcement agency interviews, the study team identified two potential operating models:

- Standard Reporting Model: Each individual financial industry entity would implement its own reporting system and report CBFT information to FinCEN consistent with acceptable electronic reporting formats.

- Hybrid Reporting Model: An entity that currently services the majority of depository institutions international funds transmittals such as the Society for Worldwide Interbank Financial Telecommunication (SWIFT) would, at the direction of its financial institution members, report CBFT information to FinCEN. Large Money Services Businesses (MSBs) would report to FinCEN on their own behalf. Small or medium MSBs would use FinCEN provided e-Filing data entry capabilities rather than implementing their own solutions.

It is important to note that these two models showcase two extremes with regards to potential operating models. In any possible future system, it is most likely that some combination of the above mentioned models could be pursued with appropriate industry and regulator input.

The differences among the operating models based on affected party include:

- Depository institutions: the benefits of the operating models appear to be limited. The costs of the Hybrid model appear to be less than the costs of the Standard model.

- MSBs: there was moderately high benefit due to a reduction in the need for compliance and legal and IT staff within the larger MSBs. The Hybrid model, moreover, reduces the impact on the smaller MSBs by shifting the cost of providing the reporting software solution to FinCEN.

- FinCEN: In the Hybrid Model FinCEN is providing the reporting software solution to smaller MSBs thereby increasing cost and effort to FinCEN. The Hybrid model also provides benefits to FinCEN since fewer help desk resources will be needed to solve data reporting issues.

- Law Enforcement: The costs and benefits are the same for both models since the data itself and the access to the data are the same.

For both operating models:

- Law enforcement and industry were in agreement that reporting on a weekly basis was reasonable.

- To reduce costs, some industry representatives recommended that all CBFT transactions be reported, not just those in excess of the $3,000 recordkeeping threshold.[2] Others indicated that this would increase costs and that further reducing the scope of any reporting requirement would reduce its cost to the industry.

Benefits to Law Enforcement and Regulatory Agencies

A range of governmental agencies regularly request from the financial industry, under their respective legal authorities, CBFT records maintained in accordance with FinCEN's recordkeeping requirement. From its interviews with law enforcement and regulatory agencies, the study team developed the following primary impact areas, also known as "business use cases":

- Terrorist Financing
- Money Laundering
- Narcotics/Contraband/Human Trafficking
- Government Sanctions/Targeted Financial Measures
- Tax Evasion
- Individual Fraud

---

[2] Changes to Section 21 of the Federal Deposit Insurance Act (12 U.S.C. § 103.33 (e) and (f) (the Funds Transfer Rule) and the 31 C.F.R. § 103.33 (g) (the travel rule), would require a joint determination of the Board of Governors of the Federal Reserve System and the Secretary of the Treasury as to the necessity of such a change. Section 6302 provides that information required to be reported under that section shall not exceed the information already required to be retained by financial institutions pursuant to the Funds Transfer Rule and the travel rule unless:

 i) The Board of Governors of the Federal Reserve System (Board) and the Secretary jointly determine that particular items of information are not currently required to be retained under those law and regulations; and

 ii) The Secretary determines, after consultation with the Board, that the reporting of such additional information is reasonably necessary to conduct the efforts of the Secretary to identify cross-border money laundering and terrorist financing.

- Market Stability and Oversight

Using our authority under the record keeping rule, FinCEN received a limited sample of CBFT data from several large financial institutions. Based on the business use cases, the study group performed an analysis of the sample data. This analysis yielded several findings:

- CBFT data fields, under current recordkeeping requirements, are sufficient to conduct the type of analyses illustrated in the business use cases, although additional fields could add value

- Upon implementation, CBFT data would immediately be available to conduct the type of analyses illustrated in the business use cases

- Having CBFT data for transactions under $3,000 would significantly benefit the type of analysis illustrated in the business use cases

- The quality of the data in the sample was found to be acceptable to conduct the type of analyses illustrated in the business use cases

- A comparison of a three month limited sample of CBFT data to FinCEN cases revealed hundreds of instances where CBFT transactions were matched with existing cases and/or pointed to additional investigative leads

Implications to the Financial Industry

The study team surveyed 279 financial institutions with 81 providing responses to FinCEN on the implications and benefits of a potential CBFT reporting requirement based upon the transactions currently subject to FinCEN's recordkeeping requirement with a $3,000 threshold. Key findings from the CBFT Survey of Financial Industry Entities include the following:

- Respondents expected an increase in the cost of complying with the new reporting requirement as compared to costs under the current process of complying with subpoenas or other legal demands under current recordkeeping requirements.

- Respondents suggested many alternative reporting methods and implementation approaches to reduce the potential costs of a reporting requirement, such as reporting CBFT data weekly or monthly, having FinCEN obtain CBFT information directly from a financial industry entity that currently services the majority of depository institutions international funds transmittals such as the Society for Worldwide Interbank Financial Telecommunication (SWIFT) or some other centralized repository, either expanding or further limiting which CBFT transactions would need to be reported, or accepting the data in the existing format used by financial institutions.

- Respondents consider customer privacy a significant concern.

- Respondents noted that the security and uses of CBFT data are also a significant concern for financial institutions, especially the perceived ease of accessibility of the data to law enforcement.

- Respondents felt that outreach and guidance both before and after the implementation of a reporting requirement would be critical to its effective implementation; this would include providing clear and specific regulations, detailed technical requirements, published guidance and frequently asked questions, sufficient implementation time, and coordinated testing opportunities.

Costs of Business Operating Models

As a part of the study, the study team developed rough order of magnitude (ROM) costs for each of the operating models. These figures represent the entire cost for implementing the solution and the annual recurring operating costs for the financial industry.[3]

Table ES-1 illustrates the average one-time implementation cost and the average recurring annual cost for each of the potential reporting models for depository institutions and MSBs.

The counts of the financial institutions in the table below are based on the conclusions of the Feasibility Study where it was determined that it was feasible to collect data from those U.S. financial institutions that transmit electronic funds instructions directly to a non-U.S. financial institution or conversely, those that received such instructions directly from a non-U.S. financial institution. Those institutions that fall outside of this definition were not included in the analysis as they would not be a part of a potential reporting requirement.

Table ES-1					
		Standard Reporting Model		**Hybrid Reporting Model**	
Type	**Size**	**Average One-Time Implementation Cost**	**Average Recurring Annual Cost**	**Average One-Time Implementation Cost**	**Average Recurring Annual Cost**
Depository Institutions	Large (5)	$249,787	$82,409	$0	$93,503
	Medium (92)	$249,787	$82,409	$0	$20,101
	Small (150)	$61,875	$59,526	$0	$6,753
MSBs	Large (6)	$250,006	$51,934	$250,006	$51,934
	Medium/Small (693)	$0	$60,000	$64	$395

Table ES-1 Comparison of the Costs of the Operating Models

Based on the results of their ROM cost analysis, the study team developed the following conclusions:

- The Hybrid Reporting Model significantly reduces the cost of a potential reporting requirement for depository institutions because the depository institutions would only incur annual reporting charges from SWIFT.

---

[3] As part of this study, estimates of FinCEN costs were developed; they are, however, not reported here because they are part of the deliberative budget process.

— The Hybrid Reporting Model significantly reduces the cost of a potential reporting requirement to MSBs, in aggregate, because the one-time and recurring annual costs of small/medium size MSBs using FinCEN's e-File data entry capabilities would be significantly less than the one-time and recurring annual costs of implementing/operating individual solutions. The costs to large MSBs would be the same under both models.

— The Hybrid Reporting Model slightly increases the costs of supporting a potential reporting requirement for FinCEN because of the higher implementation and maintenance/operation costs for the interface to SWIFT and the e-Filing CBFT data entry capabilities for small/medium size MSBs.

— Under both the Standard and Hybrid Reporting Models the cost to law enforcement agencies is the same.

Implementation Time Line

Should a CBFT reporting requirement ultimately be established, it is unlikely that CBFT reporting would begin until Fiscal Year (FY) 2011. The implementation of any potential CBFT reporting requirement would be complex, and depend upon a number of other important factors including:

- The initial approval to proceed with a rulemaking process for a CBFT reporting requirement.
- The timing of the Treasury Department's certification to Congress, as required by statute, that FinCEN has successfully deployed the system changes needed to support the receipt, processing and access to the CBFT data.
- The timing of the implementation of final regulations establishing a CBFT reporting requirement.

Security and Privacy Protection of CBFT Data

If the reporting requirement is implemented, FinCEN recognizes that CBFT data represents a large volume of information being reported to FinCEN and then made accessible to certain law enforcement and regulatory agencies. FinCEN also recognizes that there is a high degree of sensitivity regarding the security and privacy of this data.

FinCEN's overall IT modernization effort was developed with a potential CBFT reporting requirement in mind, and this effort incorporates state-of-the-art and government best practices for information security and privacy. FinCEN's CBFT data collection, warehousing and dissemination architecture would make full use of these key security and privacy controls practices (e.g., role based security access to data). In addition, FinCEN would limit access to the data to those with a need to know, specifically, financial specialists within law enforcement and regulatory agencies.

Next Steps

This study was completed to inform a policy decision whether to pursue a CBFT regulatory reporting requirement. If a decision is made to require regulatory reporting, going forward would involve the following activities:

- Initiate the rule making process

- Certify to Congress that the IT systems have been properly developed
- Publish the CBFT reporting requirement final rule
- Begin accepting CBFT data from the industry on the CBFT Final Rule effective date and making it available to appropriate law enforcement and regulatory agencies

Table of Contents

Appendices

1. Introduction

1.1 Establishing a Limited Cross-Border Funds Transmittal Reporting Requirement

Section 6302 of the Intelligence Reform and Terrorism Prevention Act of 2004 amended the BSA to require, among other things, that the Secretary of the Treasury study the feasibility of "requiring such financial institutions as the Secretary determines to be appropriate to report to the Financial Crimes Enforcement Network certain cross-border electronic transmittals of funds, if the Secretary determines that reporting of such transmittals is reasonably necessary to conduct the efforts of the Secretary against money laundering and terrorist financing." [4]

Under current FinCEN regulation, 31 C.F.R. § 103.33 (the "recordkeeping rule")[5], financial institutions are generally required to collect and retain records of certain specified data regarding funds transfers they process of $3,000 or more. Because the recordkeeping rule does not distinguish between domestic and international funds transfers, financial institutions must make and maintain records on all transmittals of at least $3,000. Further, the rule states that while institutions need not retain the information in any particular manner, their records must be in a format that is retrievable. The recordkeeping rule does not require financial institutions to report to the Financial Crimes Enforcement Network (FinCEN) the information they maintain, but only requires that the data be available upon request to FinCEN, to law enforcement, and to regulators to whom FinCEN has delegated Bank Secrecy Act (BSA) compliance examination authority through the examination process.

Prior to prescribing any such regulations, however, the Treasury Department is required: to report to Congress regarding what cross-border information would be reasonably necessary to combat money laundering and terrorist financing; to outline the criteria to be used in determining which situations require reporting; to outline the form, manner, and frequency of reporting; and to identify the technology necessary for FinCEN to store, analyze, protect, and disseminate the data collected.

To meet these requirements, FinCEN completed a study in October 2006 that assessed the overall feasibility of establishing a limited cross-border funds transmittal reporting requirement for certain financial institutions. In October 2007, FinCEN began further study of this area with the information presented in this report.

This study will be used to inform Treasury leadership and assist in their decision-making process. Under Section 6302, certification to Congress on the implementation of the technology to support Cross-Border Funds Transfer (CBFT) reporting must be accomplished prior to FinCEN prescribing the final regulatory framework.

1.2 Study Scope

This study analyzed the implications of CBFT reporting on a portion of the U.S. financial services industry and the benefits to law enforcement of having access to CBFT data. The study team sought answers to the following questions:

---

[4] Public Law No.108-458 (December 17, 2004), codified at 31 U.S.C. § 5318(n).

[5] See Section 31 C.F.R. § 103.33, Records to be made and maintained by financial institutions.

- What technical solution would be required to support FinCEN's collection and use of CBFT data and what would be the costs to FinCEN of implementing this technology?

- If certain CBFT data were reported to FinCEN, what would be the known or potential uses of this information?

- What would be the effects on the affected U.S. financial services industry of a limited CBFT reporting requirement?

- How would the security and privacy of CBFT data be protected by FinCEN?

1.3 Key Activities

To accomplish this study, FinCEN engaged in the following activities:

- Surveyed the potentially affected U.S. financial services industry (hereafter referred to as "financial institutions") to identify and, where possible, assess the effects of a potential CBFT reporting requirement

  – Solicited input on survey questions and key issues from members of the Bank Secrecy Act Advisory Group (BSAAG) Cross-Border Wire Transfer Subcommittee [6]

  – Engaged an independent survey firm to administer the survey, analyze the results, and provide summary of those results and analysis

  – Distributed the survey to 279 financial institutions

  – Conducted follow-up interviews of select survey respondents

- Interviewed law enforcement, regulatory agencies, and foreign financial intelligence units and worked with them to identify examples of how the data could be used. The following organizations were interviewed for this study:

  – U.S. Department of Justice

    • Drug Enforcement Administration

    • Federal Bureau of Investigation

    • Bureau of Alcohol, Tobacco, Firearms, and Explosives

  – U.S. Department of Homeland Security

    • U.S. Customs and Border Protection

    • U.S. Immigration and Customs Enforcement

    • U.S. Secret Service

  – U.S. Department of the Treasury

    • Financial Crimes Enforcement Network

    • Internal Revenue Service Criminal Investigation

---

[6] The Annunzio-Wylie Anti-Money Laundering Act of 1992 authorized the Secretary of the Treasury to establish the Bank Secrecy Act Advisory Group (the BSAAG) as a forum for the financial services industry, law enforcement, and regulators to advise the Secretary on ways to enhance the usefulness of BSA reporting. Since 1994, the Advisory Group has served as a forum for these groups to communicate regarding the uses of Suspicious Activity Reports, Currency Transaction Reports, and other BSA reports, and how recordkeeping and reporting requirements can be improved. The BSAAG utilizes a variety of subcommittees to identify and analyze relevant issues, including cross-border wire transfers and FinCEN's IT efforts.

- Internal Revenue Service Small Business/Self -Employed
- Office of Foreign Assets Control
  - Federal Regulatory Agencies
    - U.S. Securities and Exchange Commission
  - State Law Enforcement
    - Office of the Attorney General of Arizona
- Analyzed data samples from several financial institutions to evaluate the usability of the data
- Developed a rough order of magnitude cost estimate for the technology required to support CBFT

1.4   Organization of Document

This report presents the results of this study in the following sections:

- Section 2: Background
- Section 3: Existing and Potential Operating Models
- Section 4: Benefits to Law Enforcement and Regulatory Agencies
- Section 5: Implications to the Financial Industry
- Section 6: Costs of Implementation
- Section 7: Information Security and Privacy Controls

2. Background

2.1 Financial Crimes Enforcement Network (FinCEN)

FinCEN is a bureau within the Department of the Treasury and is the financial intelligence unit of the United States. Its mission is to enhance U.S. national security, deter and detect criminal activity, and safeguard financial systems from abuse by promoting transparency in the U.S. and international financial systems. As administrator of the BSA, FinCEN is responsible for managing, analyzing, safeguarding, and appropriately sharing information about reported financial transactions.

FinCEN was created in 1990 by order of the Secretary of the Treasury. The Secretary of the Treasury has delegated authority to FinCEN to administer the BSA. In May 1994, FinCEN's mission was broadened to include regulatory responsibilities and Treasury's Office of Financial Enforcement was merged with FinCEN. Upon enactment of the USA PATRIOT Act in October 2001,[7] Section 310 made FinCEN a Treasury bureau.

In order to fulfill its mission, FinCEN relies heavily on the use of BSA data, which is its primary and most important information asset. FinCEN collects over 17 million BSA forms and reports each year and currently maintains ten years of history available on-line. Data older than ten years are archived and available off-line. FinCEN's information technology systems integrate the collection, storage, analysis, and dissemination of the data to federal, state, and local partners. As part of FinCEN's international collaboration efforts, FinCEN may share certain information with other financial intelligence units around the world to support their respective law enforcement investigations.

2.2 Feasibility Study

In 2006, FinCEN conducted a study of the feasibility of CBFT reporting. This was required by Section 6302 of the Intelligence Reform and Terrorism Prevention Act of 2004.

The study concluded that it would be feasible to establish a limited CBFT reporting requirement for certain financial institutions. The study examined potential technology solutions for FinCEN and recommended building a federated data architecture that would be largely separate from FinCEN's existing information technology systems. Under this assumption, that report determined that it would require approximately three and one-half years and cost an estimated $32.6 million for FinCEN to implement any reporting regime. (Since that report was issued, and due to current system architecture assumptions, this figure has been revised significantly downward.)

In addition, the study concluded that the basic information already obtained and maintained by U.S. financial institutions (banks and non-bank financial institutions) pursuant to the Funds Transfer "Recordkeeping" Rule, including the $3,000 recordkeeping threshold, provides a sufficient basis for meaningful data analysis. The study stated that any reporting requirement

---

[7] Uniting and Strengthening America by Providing Appropriate Tools Required to Intercept and Obstruct Terrorism Act of 2001

should apply only to those U.S. financial institutions that exchange payment instructions directly with foreign institutions, and that the $3,000 recordkeeping threshold should apply only to discrete transactions and not to the aggregated total value of multiple transactions conducted very closely to one another in time.

Based on the recommendation of the Feasibility Study to only collect information from the first-in/last-out financial institutions, FinCEN estimates that the number of financial institutions affected would be approximately 1,000 financial institutions, which is a relatively small proportion of all U.S.-based financial institutions including both depository institutions (300) and money transmitters (700).

Finally, the study proposed a multi-phased development process. The first phase was to involve these efforts:

- Conduct a requirements analysis to determine the functionality required to meet the needs of those who access BSA data.

- Engage in discussions with financial industry representatives that would be subject to the proposed requirements along with representatives of major payment systems and members of the Canadian and Australian financial industry. These discussions would focus on quantifying the costs that the proposed requirement would impose on the reporting institutions and the potential impact on their day-to-day operations.

- Analyze fund transmittal data and explore means of extracting value from the data.

3. Existing and Potential Operating Models

One of the objectives of this study is to analyze the potential implications of CBFT reporting on the financial industry and the benefits to law enforcement of having access to the resultant data. To do this, the study team documented how CBFT data is currently disclosed to law enforcement and how it could be transmitted to FinCEN and disclosed to law enforcement should a CBFT reporting requirement be implemented.

The following sections describe the existing and potential operating models for providing CBFT data as well as the principles, assumptions, and constraints that guided the development of the potential operating models.

3.1 Existing Operating Model

Based on financial industry survey responses and interviews with financial institutions and law enforcement agencies, the study team identified the existing operating model for the disclosure of CBFT information by financial institutions to law enforcement agencies. In the existing operating model, the CBFT information disclosure process begins with the development of the investigative subpoena by law enforcement agencies for data that is maintained by financial institutions under the existing recordkeeping obligations. These operations generally:

- Are manually intensive and rely heavily on human resources to execute business processes
- Use minimal and simple types of technology to request, package, and transfer information between financial institutions and law enforcement agencies
- Employ varying security and privacy controls among the financial institutions and federal, state, and local law enforcement agencies
- Generate a unique CBFT information output format/content for each subpoena coming from federal, state, or local law enforcement agencies
- Typically are an iterative process to ensure that the law enforcement request is fully satisfied
- Involve no central coordination of data requested (e.g., by field offices of a single agency)
- Are often broad requests that overlap with other requests
- Involve the use of the requested data that is often compartmentalized by each case and is frequently overlooked for strategic analysis

The study team attempted to quantify the level of staff resources (e.g., number of staff, staff hours) expended by law enforcement agencies and financial institutions to execute the existing operating model. The study team found that this information is not readily available and that providing that data would take a significant effort on the part of law enforcement agencies and financial institutions.

3.1.1 Existing Operating Model – Law Enforcement Agencies

Based on interviews with law enforcement agencies, the study team found that law enforcement agencies generally:

- Use leads and/or other case information to try to determine the characteristics and identifiers of the CBFT information that may be relevant to an investigation. This is a highly manual process and investigative subpoenas may be written broadly to mitigate the need for additional subpoenas. The result of this approach is that requests for CBFT information may be more extensive than necessary in order to ensure that critical information is not missed and the process for a new subpoena must be initiated.

- Require a team of information analysts, agents/investigators, and legal counsel to develop, review, and communicate the subpoena and supporting detail to financial institutions.

- Use varying encryption and communication channels to request and receive CBFT information from financial institutions, resulting in uneven application of security and privacy controls.

- Use additional law enforcement human resources once the CBFT information output is received from financial institutions to manually enter and/or transfer the information into simple technology tools (e.g., spreadsheets, desktop databases), before data analysis can begin.

- Are creating duplicative databases based on CBFT data obtained through subpoenas

3.1.2 Existing Operating Model – Financial Industry Entities

Based on financial industry survey responses and follow-up interviews with financial institutions, the study team found that financial institutions generally:

- Require a team of compliance and legal staff to receive, assess, and determine appropriate action for each subpoena from law enforcement agencies, both for the initial request for information and subsequent requests for clarifying/additional information.

- Rely on a team of information technology staff to develop a unique CBFT data query and output format (report or file) for each subpoena from law enforcement agencies.

- Use commonly available tools to transfer data to law enforcement (e.g., spreadsheets, desktop databases, text files).

3.2 Principles, Assumptions, and Constraints for the Potential Operating Model

This section provides the principles, assumptions, and constraints that were used in developing the potential operating model for disclosing CBFT information to law enforcement agencies under a CBFT reporting requirement.

3.2.1 Principles

The study team identified three principles for the development of the potential operating model:

- The potential CBFT requirement is focused on reporting transactions; therefore, the potential operating model would not require changes to the processes or technology used by financial institutions to execute cross-border funds transmittals.

- The potential operating model will focus on automating and standardizing the reporting of CBFT information by financial institutions to FinCEN and the access to the information by law enforcement agencies.

- The potential operating model will address CBFT information security and privacy concerns, both in the reporting of information by financial institutions and the access to the information by law enforcement agencies.

3.2.2 Assumptions

The development of the potential operating models are based on the following assumptions:

- The CBFT operating model environment begins after the financial institutions complete their CBFT process and the CBFT data is available for reporting.

- The CBFT information reporting process begins with the transmission of CBFT data to FinCEN. For the potential operating model, the process would conclude where the existing operating model concludes now, at the point where law enforcement agencies can begin their analysis of the CBFT data.

- CBFTs will be electronically submitted. FinCEN will provide a registered user portal for financial institutions to use for reporting a CBFT via e-File data entry. Paper forms will generally not be accepted by FinCEN.

- Law enforcement agencies will use pre-established channels to access CBFT information managed by FinCEN.

- The potential operating model will rely on the security and privacy controls implemented for financial institutions and law enforcement agencies in the FinCEN IT environment. (See Appendix A, FinCEN IT Information Security and Privacy Controls)

- Form and regulation changes will follow the rule making process and align with the selected potential operating model.

3.3 Potential Operating Models

After analyzing the existing operating model, financial industry survey responses, and input gathered during financial institution and law enforcement agency interviews, the study team identified two potential operating models for use in this analysis.

The two operating models analyzed in this study include:

- Standard Reporting Model: Each individual financial institution implements its own reporting system and reports CBFT information to FinCEN. This model is the closest to the current process.

- Hybrid Reporting Model: The Society for Worldwide Interbank Financial Telecommunication (SWIFT) [8] reports CBFT information to FinCEN at the direction of its financial institution members. Large Money Services Businesses (MSB) will report to FinCEN on their own behalf and small/medium MSBs will use FinCEN provided e-Filing data entry capabilities rather than implementing their own solutions.

---

[8] The Society for Worldwide Interbank Financial Telecommunication (SWIFT), a cooperative society owned by its member financial institutions, is a unified international electronic financial transaction messaging service. FinCEN does not endorse commercial service providers. SWIFT is used here as a representative example of a financial institution CBFT reporting agent because banks identified it overwhelmingly as the primary vehicle for sending CBFT instructions.

FinCEN recognizes that there may be other options; for example, even if the Hybrid model were to be pursued, depository institutions could still opt-out of using SWIFT as their data provider and submit the data directly to FinCEN.

In both of the potential operating models, the study team sought to reduce the effort of financial institutions and increase investigative efficiency of law enforcement by:

- Reducing the number and scope of investigative subpoenas and requests for clarifying information sent from law enforcement agencies to financial institutions
- Reducing financial institution and law enforcement agency human resources required to execute business processes
- Increasing the use of technology to automate and standardize the transfer of data between financial institutions, FinCEN, and law enforcement agencies
- Employing consistent security and privacy controls between the financial institutions, FinCEN, and law enforcement agencies
- Reducing the number of overlapping requests and increasing the use of data obtained from financial institutions

The study team attempted to quantify the potential reduction in staff resources (number of staff, staff hours) expended by law enforcement agencies and financial institutions that could result from the adoption of the potential operating model. As mentioned earlier, current information was not readily available for the existing operating model, making comparisons from the existing to either of the two potential operating models not possible.

3.3.1 Standard Reporting Model

In the Standard Reporting Model, each individual financial institution implements its own reporting system and reports CBFT information to FinCEN. Figure 3-1 depicts, at a high level, the potential business processes and technology used to request, package, and transfer information between law enforcement agencies and financial institutions.

Standard Reporting Model

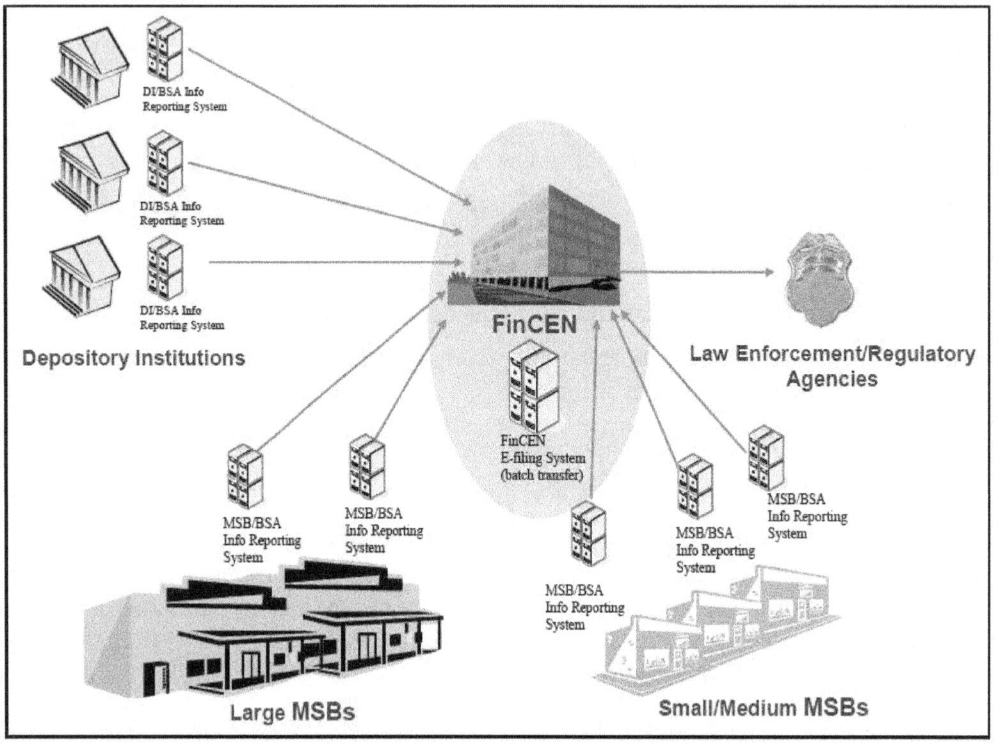

Figure 3-1 Standard Reporting Model - Flow of CBFT Data

3.3.1.1   Standard Reporting Model – Law Enforcement Agencies

Based on interviews with law enforcement agencies, the study team designed the potential operating model to help law enforcement agencies:

- Improve their ability to retrieve only the most relevant CBFT information for data analysis by incorporating more sophisticated data query and decision analytics tools that minimize the retrieval of excess data.

- Reduce the number of initial and subsequent investigative subpoenas used to obtain CBFT information from financial institutions, and therefore the level of human resources from information analysts, agents/investigators, and legal counsel needed to develop, review, and communicate subpoenas and their supporting information request details. Note that while the number and the frequency of these complex CBFT data subpoenas should be reduced, the number of specifically targeted subpoenas may increase (e.g., subpoenas needed to obtain related non-CBFT account information or expert witnesses for trial testimony).

- Use consistent encryption and secure communication channels to request/receive CBFT information from FinCEN, resulting in the standard application of security and privacy controls.

- Reduce the use of additional law enforcement human resources once CBFT information is received by incorporating the use of more sophisticated, automated extract/transform/load tools before data analysis begins.

- Reduce duplicative databases maintained by individual law enforcement agencies.

3.3.1.2 Standard Reporting Model – Financial Industry Entities

Based on financial industry survey responses and follow-up interviews with financial institutions, the study team designed the potential operating model to help financial institutions:

- Reduce the number of initial and subsequent subpoenas received from law enforcement agencies to obtain CBFT information, and therefore the level of human resources from compliance and legal staff needed to receive, assess, and determine appropriate action for each of those subpoenas. Based on survey follow-up interviews, financial institutions for which CBFTs are a significant portion of their business asserted that they expected to see a significant reduction in the number and frequency of subpoenas used to initially obtain data for investigative purposes and a reduction in the use of human resources to respond to these investigative subpoenas. Those financial institutions for which CBFTs are a small portion of their business should not expect to see a significant reduction in subpoenas for investigative purposes because the subpoenas generally also request bank statement or other customer information as well as CBFT information. The number of targeted subpoenas needed to support specific prosecutions is not expected to significantly change.

- Reduce the use of information technology human resources to develop a unique CBFT data query and output format (report or file) for each subpoena from law enforcement agencies and to respond to subsequent information requests.

- Employ more sophisticated technology to extract/transform/transmit CBFT information to FinCEN.

- Use consistent encryption and communication channels to transmit CBFT information to FinCEN, resulting in the standard application of security and privacy controls.

3.3.2 Hybrid Reporting Model

The Hybrid Reporting Model is based on the depository institutions use of a financial industry entity that currently services the majority of depository institutions' international funds transmittals (e.g., SWIFT) to collect CBFT instructions from depository institutions. As indicated in the Feasibility Study and as confirmed through the industry survey, SWIFT is the primary method for international funds transmittal messages by depository institutions.

Survey respondents also recommended that FinCEN explore the possibility of the depository institutions instructing SWIFT to make copies of the funds transfer instructions, to alleviate the depository institution from having to create a unique information technology solution.

MSBs generally use proprietary systems for transmitting payment orders. Under this reporting model, each MSB reports to FinCEN on its own behalf, with large MSBs using FinCEN's e-file batch transfer capabilities while small and medium-size MSBs will be provided with FinCEN's e-File data entry capabilities rather than implementing their own reporting systems.

Figure 3-2 depicts, at a high level, the Hybrid Reporting Model with the potential business processes and technology used to request, package, and transfer information among law enforcement, financial institutions and FinCEN.

3.3.2.1 Hybrid Reporting Model – Law Enforcement Agencies

The key attributes for law enforcement agencies of this operating model are the same as for the Standard reporting model.

Hybrid Reporting Model

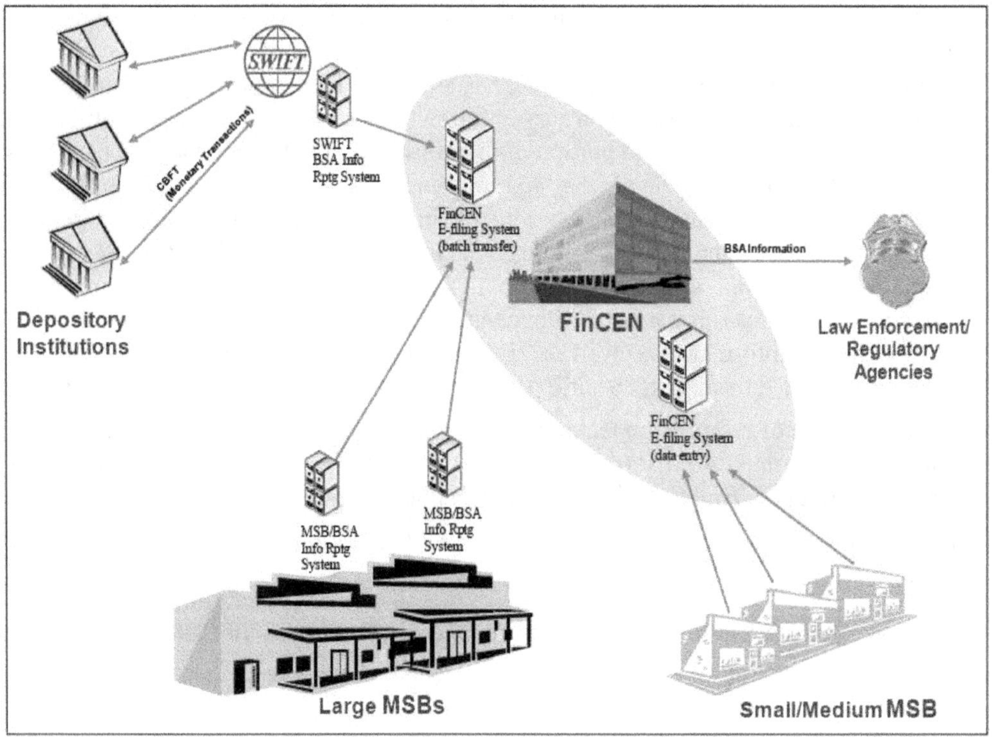

Figure 3-2 Hybrid Reporting Model – Flow of CBFT Data

3.3.2.2 Hybrid Reporting Model – Financial Industry Entities

For those financial institutions that are depository institutions, the study team designed this model to:

- Reduce the duplication of information technology human resources by allowing institutions to instruct a company agent (e.g., SWIFT) to transmit their CBFT information to FinCEN.
- Rely on the same security and privacy controls that they do in sending the transaction instructions via SWIFT.

For those financial institutions that are MSBs, the study team designed this model to:

- Provide the same key attributes as the Standard reporting model.

- Reduce reporting implementation and recurring costs for small and medium-size MSBs by using reporting systems provided by FinCEN.

4. Benefits to Law Enforcement and Regulatory Agencies

4.1 Introduction

In accordance with Section 6302 of the Intelligence Reform and Terrorism Prevention Act of 2004, this study was undertaken to help determine if "reporting of such transmittals is reasonably necessary to conduct the efforts of the Secretary against money laundering and terrorist financing." In order to demonstrate the "reasonable necessity" of the data collected in CBFT transactions, the study team worked with law enforcement and regulatory agencies to identify how CBFT data would be usable for those identified purposes.

The results of that analysis are presented as follows:

- Section 4.2, Business Use Case Process, describes the study team's approach to developing the business use cases which illustrate potential uses of the data.

- Section 4.3, Categories of Analysis, explains how the use cases were categorized (e.g., reactive, proactive).

- Section 4.4, Domestic Business Use Case Summary, summarizes the use cases that the study team developed.

- Section 4.5, Use of CBFT Data by International Financial Intelligence Units (FIUs), summarizes the use of CBFT data by FinCEN's counterpart FIUs in foreign countries.

- Section 4.6, Data Usability, Quality, and Prototyping presents the results of the study team's analysis to validate the usability of the data with CBFT data samples provided by the financial industry.

4.2 The Business Use Case Process

To conduct its business use analysis, FinCEN first identified thirteen different federal and state law enforcement and regulatory agencies that likely would benefit from access to CBFT data based upon their investigative mission, current use of BSA data, or existing utilization of CBFT data obtained from financial institutions. During a series of comprehensive interviews with those agencies, law enforcement and regulatory agency representatives identified how they could utilize the data collected in CBFT transactions to support their investigative missions. The results of the interviews, presented in this study as business use cases, demonstrate how access to CBFT data could improve both the efficiency of these agencies' current investigations and their ability to identify new investigative targets.

Through the development of detailed, individualized business use cases, the study team has expanded on the related preliminary analytical efforts and investigative methods outlined in the Feasibility Study. While the study team was able to expand on those earlier efforts to identify a number of specific business use cases involving CBFT data, the report showcases only those examples most supportive of each agency's unique mission.

The study team conducted business use case interviews with the following agencies:

US Department of Justice	**US Department of Homeland Security**	**US Department of the Treasury**	**Federal Regulatory Agencies**	**State Law Enforcement**
• Bureau of Alcohol, Tobacco, Firearms and Explosives	• US Customs and Border Protection	• Financial Crimes Enforcement Network	• US Securities and Exchange Commission	• Office of the Attorney General of Arizona
• Drug Enforcement Administration	• US Immigration and Customs Enforcement	• Internal Revenue Service Criminal Investigation		
• Federal Bureau of Investigation	• US Secret Service	• Internal Revenue Service Small Business/ Self Employed		
		• Office of Foreign Assets Control		

FinCEN, as the FIU of the United States, also contacted representatives from multiple international FIUs to identify benefits those countries have realized from the use of cross-border funds transmittal data. The contacted FIUs stated that there was significant value to their investigative missions in having access to CBFT data, as well as a benefit to broader international efforts to fight financial crimes (see Section 4.5). These FIUs also provided official correspondence to FinCEN detailing their responses (see Appendix B).

4.3   Categories of Analysis

During the business use case interview process, agency representatives classified their analyses into two distinct categories: Reactive or Proactive analysis.

- Reactive analysis is a targeted analytical process designed to identify additional information on a known subject of interest. For example, an agent or analyst would query a subject's name or identification number through a series of databases to identify financial, law enforcement, and commercially available information to support an investigation (see figure 4-1).

- Proactive analysis is an analytical process designed to identify new subjects of interest engaged in a specific type or pattern of illicit activity, such as terrorist financing, money laundering, or tax evasion. For example, an agent or analyst may conduct proactive analysis of CBFT data to identify a list of subjects potentially engaged in the exploitation of offshore tax havens. Based upon an analysis of any geographic information contained in CBFT transactions, an agent or analyst may be able to identify subjects potentially seeking to transmit taxable income from the United States to known offshore tax havens. After identifying an initial group of potential subjects, an agent or analyst would query these subjects through additional databases to refine the list based on newly identified information. The analysis will result in a high-priority list of subjects suspected of engaging in a specific type or pattern of illicit activity (see figure 4-2).

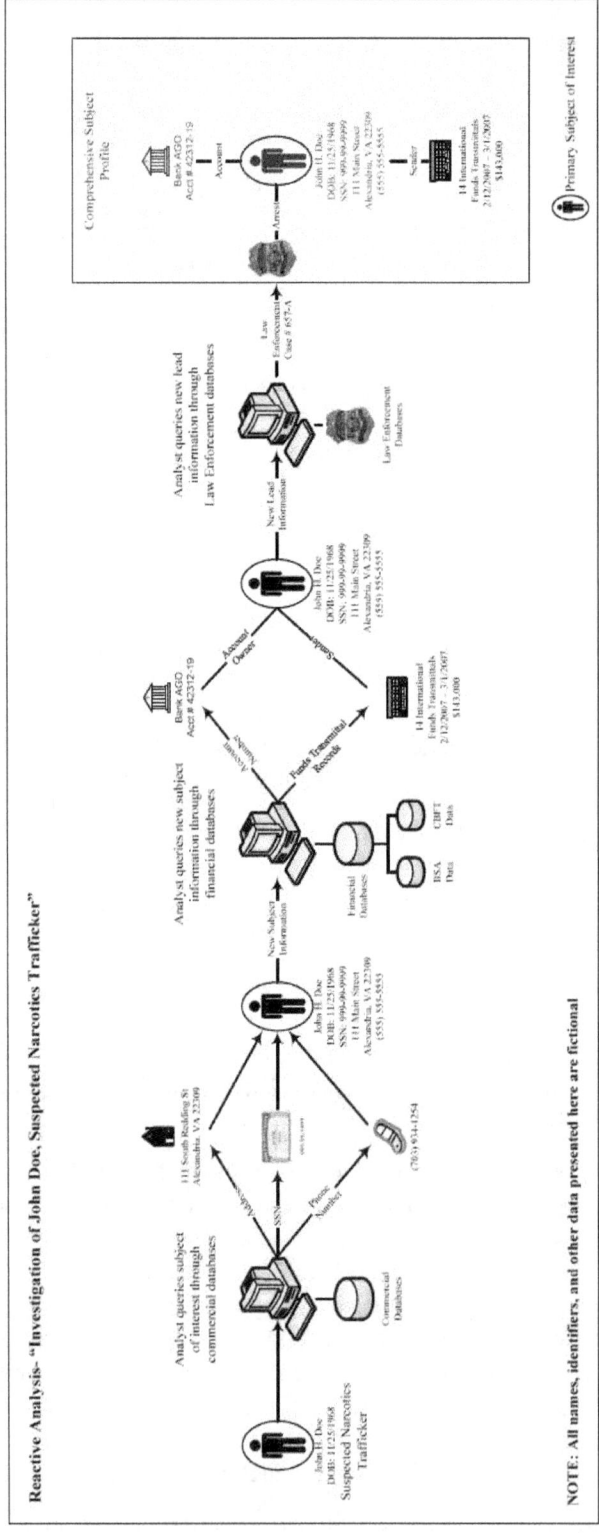

Figure 4-1 Reactive Analytical Process

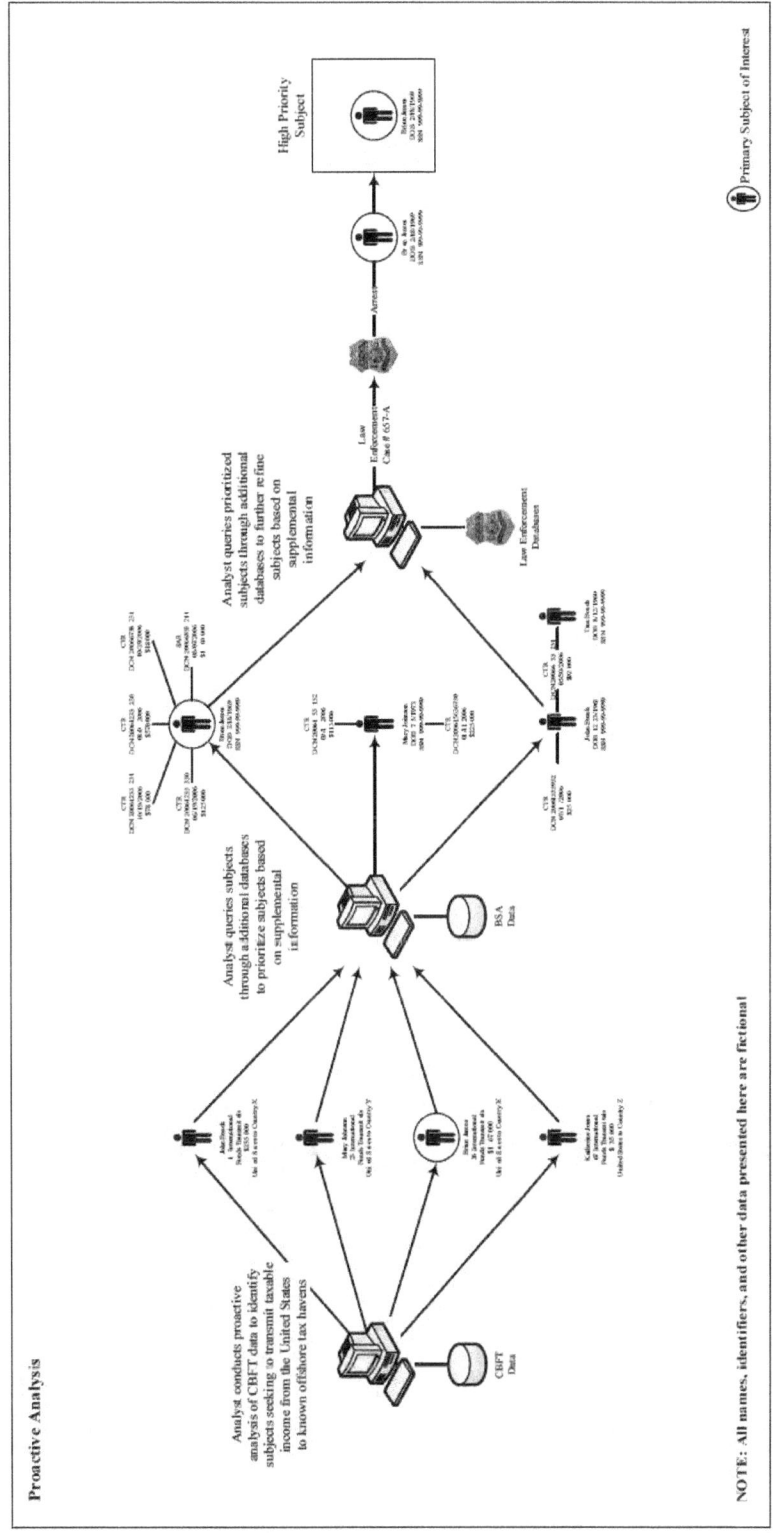

Figure 4-2 Proactive Analytical Process

4.4 Domestic Business Use Case Summaries

To demonstrate the practical value of data collected in CBFT transactions, law enforcement and regulatory agencies identified twenty-two business use cases within seven major investigative categories:

- Terrorist Financing
- Money Laundering
- Narcotics/Contraband/Human Trafficking
- Government Sanctions/Targeted Financial Measures
- Tax Evasion
- Individual Fraud
- Market Stability and Oversight

These cases are not meant to be exhaustive, but rather to be indicative of the broad range of law enforcement potential uses of CBFT data.

Throughout the business use case process, law enforcement and regulatory agencies indicated that in many of the core criminal activities under their jurisdiction, from terrorist financing to human trafficking, there is an international financial element. The availability of CBFT data would give law enforcement and regulatory agencies investigating these activities access to key data elements in CBFT transactions at the earliest, and often the most critical, stages of their investigations.

The business use case process also illustrated the potential complementary value of CBFT and BSA data in the detection of illicit financial activity. By combining information contained in Suspicious Activity Reports (SARs) and Currency Transactions Reports (CTRs) with key data elements contained in CBFT transactions, such as names, addresses, and account numbers, the business use cases demonstrate how access to CBFT and BSA data could potentially improve the ability of law enforcement and regulatory agencies to detect, disrupt, and dismantle illicit activity.

The following table summarizes the business use cases. Full use cases were developed during the course of the study however these have not been included in this report because their publication could aid criminals in their attempts to avoid detection.

Agency	Type	Use Case Title
Terrorist Financing		
Federal Bureau of Investigation (FBI)	Reactive	Terrorist Financing Investigations
Money Laundering		
Federal Bureau of Investigation (FBI)	Proactive	Disrupting Transnational Organized Crime Syndicates
Immigration and Customs Enforcement (ICE)	Proactive	Trade-Based Money Laundering Investigations
Immigration and Customs Enforcement (ICE)	Reactive	Transnational Money Laundering Investigations
Financial Crimes Enforcement Network (FinCEN)	Reactive	Improved BSA Link Analysis Capabilities
Financial Crimes Enforcement Network (FinCEN)	Proactive	Shell Company International Fund Flow Identification
Financial Crimes Enforcement Network (FinCEN)	Proactive	Identification and Assessment of Illicit Transnational Currency Flows
Narcotics/Contraband/Human Trafficking		

Agency	Type	Use Case Title
Drug Enforcement Administration (DEA)	Reactive	Controlled Substance Investigations
Drug Enforcement Administration (DEA)	Proactive	Controlled Substance Investigations
Immigration and Customs Enforcement (ICE)	Proactive	Trade-Based Narcotics Investigations
Customs and Border Protection (CBP)	Reactive	Contraband Interdiction at United States Borders
Office of the Attorney General of Arizona	Proactive	Money Transmitter Data Related to Human Trafficking Investigations
Bureau of Alcohol, Tobacco, Firearms and Explosives (ATF)	Proactive	Disruption of Interstate Tobacco Diversion Operations
Government Sanctions/Targeted Financial Measures		
Office of Foreign Assets Control (OFAC)	Reactive	Narcotics Sanctions Investigations Pursuant to Executive Order 12978 and the Kingpin Act
Financial Crimes Enforcement Network (FinCEN)	Reactive	Special measures against entities of "Primary Money Laundering Concern" – USA PATRIOT Act Section 311 Analysis
Tax Evasion		
Internal Revenue Service Criminal Investigation (CI)	Reactive	Tax Evasion Investigations
Internal Revenue Service Small Business Self Employed (SB/SE)	Proactive	Offshore Tax Haven Abuse Investigations
Individual Fraud		
United States Secret Service (USSS)	Reactive	Identity Theft and Credit Card Fraud Investigations
Market Stability and Oversight		
United States Securities and Exchange Commission (SEC)	Reactive	Foreign Corrupt Practices Act Investigations
Financial Crimes Enforcement Network (FinCEN)	Proactive	Unregistered Money Services Businesses (MSBs) Identification
Financial Crimes Enforcement Network (FinCEN)	Proactive	Emerging High-Risk Financial Trend Identification

4.4.1 Terrorist Financing

Agency	Type	Use Case Title
Federal Bureau of Investigation (FBI)	Reactive	Terrorist Financing Investigations

Federal Bureau of Investigation (FBI)

The FBI works to defend our nation against terrorist and foreign intelligence threats and to enforce our country's federal criminal statutes. To defend our nation against terrorist and foreign intelligence threats, the FBI has established three national security priorities: counterterrorism, counterintelligence, and cybercrime. Under statutory authority granted by Title 28, United States Code, Section 533, the Attorney General has specifically assigned the FBI as the lead federal agency for investigating domestic terrorism.

Terrorist Financing Investigations

The FBI's Counterterrorism Division works with partners in the law enforcement, intelligence, military, and diplomatic communities to detect, disrupt, and dismantle terrorist cells and operatives in the United States, identify and prevent acts of terrorism by individuals with a terrorist agenda acting alone, and interdict terrorist support networks, including financial support networks, both domestically and abroad.

Building on the FBI's expertise in conducting complex criminal financial investigations and its long-established relationships with the financial services sector, the Counterterrorism Division seeks to track and shut down terrorist financing, exploit financial information to identify previously unknown terrorist cells, and recognize potential terrorist activities and planning.

To support the FBI's efforts in tracking and freezing terrorist assets, FBI analysts conduct sophisticated analysis to identify financial transactions indicative of terrorist financing. The availability of CBFT data would significantly improve the efficiency of FBI analysts investigating targets suspected of engaging in terrorist financing. Utilizing key data elements contained in CBFT transactions, such as names, addresses, and account numbers, FBI analysts would be better able to identify and track the financial structures supporting terrorist organizations; a vital component of the FBI's mission to dismantle terrorist operations and prevent future attacks. Such analysis could play a significant role in the ability of the FBI to detect, disrupt, and dismantle terrorist financial support networks.

4.4.2 Money Laundering

Agency	Type	Use Case Titles
Federal Bureau of Investigation (FBI)	Proactive	Disrupting Transnational Organized Crime Syndicates
Immigration and Customs Enforcement (ICE)	Proactive	Trade-Based Money Laundering Investigations
Immigration and Customs Enforcement (ICE)	Reactive	Transnational Money Laundering Investigations
Financial Crimes Enforcement Network (FinCEN)	Reactive	Improved BSA Link Analysis Capabilities
Financial Crimes Enforcement Network (FinCEN)	Proactive	Shell Company International Fund Flow Identification
Financial Crimes Enforcement Network (FinCEN)	Proactive	Identification and Assessment of Illicit Transnational Currency Flows

Federal Bureau of Investigation (FBI)
Disrupting Transnational Organized Crime Syndicates

One of the most significant criminal priorities of the FBI is organized crime. Transnational organized crime syndicates undermine free enterprise and raise the level of violence, fraud, and corruption in cities throughout the United States. To combat this threat, the FBI employs a range of investigative capabilities to assist in the disruption and dismantling of organized crime syndicates. Working closely with international partners, the FBI seeks to dismantle syndicates with global ties by identifying and disrupting the financial networks used to launder the proceeds generated from organized crime.

To support efforts to detect and disrupt illicit financial activity, the FBI has developed the Suspicious Activity Report (SAR) intelligence initiative. Under the initiative, FBI analysts conduct sophisticated analysis to identify emerging financial trends and patterns and disseminate new crime leads to FBI field offices throughout the United States. The initiative has enhanced the FBI's efforts to identify money laundering associated with transnational organized crime.

The availability of CBFT data would improve the ability of FBI analysts, working under the SAR intelligence initiative, to proactively identify new targets suspected of engaging in money laundering associated with organized crime. Through the analysis of key CBFT data elements, such as names and account numbers, FBI analysts would be better able to detect international networks of illicit financial activity. Such analysis could play a significant role in the ability of the FBI to disrupt and dismantle organized crime syndicates and enforce the criminal statutes of the United States.

Immigration and Customs Enforcement (ICE)

The Immigration and Customs Enforcement (ICE) division of the Department of Homeland Security (DHS) works to eliminate vulnerabilities that pose a threat to our nation's borders and to enforce economic, transportation, and infrastructure security. To achieve this mission, ICE targets the people, money, and materials that support criminal organizations and activities.

Trade-Based Money Laundering Investigations

As formal financial systems become more highly regulated and transparent, criminal entities have resorted to alternative means of moving, laundering, and storing illicit proceeds. Fraudulent practices in international commerce allow criminals to launder illicit funds while avoiding taxes, tariffs, and customs duties. To identify and eliminate customs fraud and trade-based money laundering, ICE has established Trade Transparency Units (TTU) worldwide. These TTUs have enhanced international cooperative investigative efforts to combat activities designed to exploit vulnerabilities in the United States financial and trade systems.

ICE TTUs conduct complex analysis of financial transactions in conjunction with existing United States and foreign trade data to detect money laundering activities involving the international movement of over-valued or under-valued goods. The availability of CBFT data would improve the ability of ICE analysts to proactively identify new targets suspected of engaging in trade-based money laundering. Intelligence contained in the CBFT transactions, such as originator, beneficiary, and transaction amount data, would assist ICE analysts in the identification of international financial payments indicative of the settlement of the balance of irregularly priced goods. The identification of such payments could improve the ability of ICE to dismantle the financial infrastructures of criminal organizations.

Transnational Money Laundering Investigations

To help dismantle the complex financial infrastructures used by criminal entities to move and launder funds, ICE employs sophisticated financial investigative techniques to identify the patterns and anomalies in financial transactions most indicative of financial crimes. The availability of CBFT data would significantly improve the ability of ICE agents and analysts to conduct complex financial investigations using techniques such as discrepancy analysis.

By cross-referencing key data elements contained in CBFT data, such as transaction dates and amounts, with equivalent information in BSA filings, ICE analysts would be able to identify discrepancies between the sum of CBFT activity and the sum of BSA filings during a specific timeframe for an entity under investigation. The analysis of these discrepancies would improve the ability of ICE analysts to identify unaccounted-for funds potentially associated with illicit financial activity. By using CBFT data to assist in the identification, disruption, and dismantling of the complex financial infrastructures used by criminal entities to move and launder illicit funds, ICE could be better able to enforce the laws under their jurisdiction.

Financial Crimes Enforcement Network (FinCEN)

FinCEN's mission is to enhance U.S. national security, deter and detect criminal activity, and safeguard financial systems from abuse by promoting transparency in the U.S. and international financial systems. To combat these threats, FinCEN administers the BSA which requires financial institutions to maintain appropriate records and to file reports that are used in criminal, tax, and regulatory investigations. BSA filings aid law enforcement agencies in the investigation of suspected criminal activity such as narcotics trafficking, income tax evasion, and money laundering.

Improved BSA Link Analysis Capabilities

To support law enforcement, FinCEN analysts conduct sophisticated analysis, cross-referencing multiple disparate data sources, to identify financial transactions indicative of money laundering, terrorist financing, or other illicit activity. The identification of these transactions is often dependent on the ability of FinCEN analysts to link BSA records with subjects of interest to law enforcement. Access to key data elements in CBFT data would improve this ability by providing important lead information such as names, addresses, and account numbers. By assisting FinCEN analysts link previously unidentified BSA records with subjects of interest to law enforcement, CBFT data could significantly enhance FinCEN's efforts to safeguard the financial system from the abuses of financial crime.

Shell Company International Fund Flow Identification

Criminal entities often seek to exploit vulnerabilities in the U.S. financial system, such as shell companies. By virtue of the ease of formation and the absence of ownership disclosure requirements, shell companies are attractive vehicles for those seeking to launder money or conduct illicit financial activity. While shell companies may have legitimate commercial uses, the lack of transparency in the formation process poses vulnerabilities to the financial system both domestically and abroad.

The use of shell companies as parties in international funds transmittals allows for the movement of funds by unknown beneficial owners and may be used to facilitate financial crimes such as terrorist financing and money laundering. To combat these threats, FinCEN conducts sophisticated analysis, cross-referencing multiple disparate data sources, to identify international fund movements by suspected shell companies. The availability of CBFT data would improve FinCEN's ability to identify the international movement of funds involving shell companies identified in Suspicious Activity Reports (SARs). Such analysis could play a critical role in the ability of FinCEN to support law enforcement agencies investigating criminal activity associated with shell companies.

Identification and Assessment of Illicit Transnational Currency Flows

FinCEN conducts sophisticated analysis of BSA data to provide strategic analytical support to law enforcement through the identification of trends, patterns, and issues associated with illicit financial activity. Strategic analysis products are intended to assist FinCEN's partners in the improvement of money laundering prevention and detection programs while providing support for the enforcement of anti-money laundering laws and regulations. Through the strategic analysis of BSA data, FinCEN seeks to identify newly emerging or inadequately understood money laundering methodologies, examine geographic, industry, and other systemic money laundering vulnerabilities, and provide support to federal, state, local, and international law enforcement agencies investigating complex financial crimes.

The availability of CBFT data would improve FinCEN's ability to provide strategic analytical support to law enforcement through the identification of trends, patterns, and issues associated with international funds transmittals. Through the use of location, volume, and transactional information contained in CBFT data, FinCEN analysts will be better able to identify and assess international money laundering trends and vulnerabilities. Such analysis could play a critical role in the ability of FinCEN to provide strategic support to law enforcement.

4.4.3 Narcotics/Contraband/Human Trafficking

Agency	Type	Use Case Titles
Drug Enforcement Administration (DEA)	Reactive/ Proactive	Controlled Substance Investigations
Immigration and Customs Enforcement (ICE)	Proactive	Trade-Based Narcotics Investigations
Customs and Border Protection (CBP)	Reactive	Contraband Interdiction at United States Borders
Office of the Attorney General of Arizona	Proactive	Money Transmitter Data Related to Human Trafficking Investigations
Bureau of Alcohol, Tobacco, Firearms and Explosives (ATF)	Proactive	Disruption of Interstate Tobacco Diversion Operations

Drug Enforcement Administration (DEA)

The Drug Enforcement Administration (DEA) works to disrupt and dismantle those organizations involved in the growing, manufacture, or distribution of controlled substances destined for illicit traffic in the United States. Through the investigation and preparation for prosecution of criminals, gangs, and other major violators of controlled substance laws, the DEA seeks to reduce the availability of illicit controlled substances on the domestic and international markets.

Controlled Substance Investigations

To combat the illicit trafficking of controlled substances in the United States, the DEA manages a national intelligence program to collect, analyze, and disseminate strategic and operational intelligence information about controlled substances. Such intelligence is essential to the DEA's efforts to interdict the distribution of controlled substances and disrupt and dismantle organizations that traffic in controlled substances. A critical component of these efforts is the DEA's ability to detect and deter the laundering of proceeds generated from the sale of illicit controlled substances.

To support these efforts, DEA analysts conduct sophisticated analysis to identify financial transactions indicative of controlled substance-related money laundering. DEA analysts utilize information provided by confidential informants and defendants who have entered into plea agreements to develop leads for controlled substance trafficking and controlled substance-related money laundering investigations. By cross-referencing this lead information with key data elements contained in CBFT transactions, DEA analysts would be able to more efficiently identify financial transactions indicative of the laundering of proceeds from the sale of illicit controlled substances. The availability of CBFT data would also significantly improve the ability of DEA analysts to proactively identify new targets suspected of engaging in controlled substance trafficking by tracing the flow of proceeds from the sale of illicit controlled substances to previously unknown entities and organizations. Both types of analyses could play a significant role in the ability of the DEA to interdict the distribution of controlled substances and disrupt and dismantle controlled substance trafficking organizations in the United States.

Immigration and Customs Enforcement (ICE)
Trade-Based Narcotics Investigations

ICE agents and analysts work to prevent the illicit flow of narcotics across the borders of the United States. To help identify and eliminate trade-based narcotics trafficking, ICE has established Trade Transparency Units (TTU) worldwide. These TTUs have enhanced international investigative efforts to combat narcotics trafficking activities designed to exploit vulnerabilities in the United States' financial and trade systems. Along the southern border of the United States, criminal enterprises have exploited these vulnerabilities to facilitate the illicit drug trade. To combat this threat, ICE TTUs, in conjunction with Customs authorities in several South American countries, cross-reference financial transactions with United States and foreign trade data to detect trade-based narcotics trafficking.

The availability of CBFT data would enhance the ability of ICE analysts to proactively identify new targets suspected of engaging in trade-based narcotics trafficking. By comparing key data elements contained in CBFT records, such as transaction dates and amounts, with international trade data, ICE analysts will be better able to identify payments for over-valued commodities used as compensation for the shipment of narcotics. Such analysis could improve the ability of ICE to prevent the illicit flow of narcotics into the United States.

Customs and Border Protection (CBP)

The U.S. Customs and Border Protection Agency has a number of missions, such as apprehending individuals attempting to enter the country illegally and stemming the flow of illicit drugs and contraband into the United States. CBP also works to prevent terrorists and terrorist weapons from entering the United States. To achieve this mission, CBP has established inspection sites at all ports of entry and conducts specialized secondary inspections designed to interdict individuals and contraband that may pose a threat to our nation's security.

Contraband Interdiction at United States Borders

To interdict the flow of contraband across United States borders, CBP officers conduct additional screenings of passengers that may pose a threat to our nation's security. This screening process, combined with innovative analysis of flight and financial information, aims to interdict individuals seeking to transport contraband into or out of the United States. The availability of CBFT data would enhance the ability of CBP officers to stem the flow of contraband across the borders of the United States. By cross-referencing dates and amounts contained in CBFT transactions with flight data, CBP officers would be better able to identify suspicious patterns of flight and financial activity, leading to more targeted secondary inspections of passengers potentially engaged in illicit activity.

Office of the Attorney General of Arizona

The Office of the Attorney General of Arizona has teamed with the Department of Homeland Security, the Phoenix Police Department, and the Arizona Department of Public Safety to investigate and prosecute criminal and civil racketeering/asset forfeiture cases within the state.

Money Transmitter Data Related to Human Trafficking Investigations

As the trafficking of undocumented aliens into Arizona by smugglers ("coyotes") has become more aggressive, the Financial Crimes Task Force and the Office of the Attorney General of Arizona have initiated new strategies to combat it. One key strategy has been to target the smugglers' financial underpinnings. Working with banks, courts, and state and local law enforcement agencies, the Office of the Attorney General of Arizona has targeted funds transmittals that are vital to these smuggling operations. Financial crime experts in the Attorney General's Office and the Department of Public Safety have developed cutting-edge computer algorithms to review transmittal payments sent into Arizona and to identify suspicious financial activity.

The availability of CBFT data would greatly enhance the ability of analysts from the Office of the Attorney General of Arizona to proactively identify entities suspected of engaging in human trafficking. Using intelligence derived from CBFT data fields, such as names, addresses, and telephone numbers, Office of the Attorney General of Arizona analysts would be better able to trace the illicit flow of proceeds from their domestic origin to foreign recipients. Such analysis could play a critical role in the ability of the Office of the Attorney General of Arizona to interdict organized crime associated with human and drug trafficking.

Bureau of Alcohol, Tobacco, Firearms and Explosives (ATF)

In its effort to prevent terrorism, reduce violent crime, and safeguard the United States, the Bureau of Alcohol, Tobacco, Firearms and Explosives (ATF) works to reduce crime involving firearms and explosives, acts of arson, and the illegal trafficking of alcohol and tobacco products.

Disruption of Interstate Tobacco Diversion Operations

The trafficking of contraband tobacco products is a global problem; contraband cigarettes are believed to be the number-one black market commodity in the world. There are diversion schemes occurring world-wide, and the estimates of tax loss due to diversion in the United States alone total billions of dollars each year. Through the avoidance of state and federal excise taxes, criminal organizations are able to generate enormous profits from the diversion of tobacco products. Of significant concern is the use of tobacco diversion operations to fund terrorist organizations. Since 2002, the ATF has conducted two tobacco diversion investigations resulting in the conviction of individuals for providing material support to terrorist organizations.

In order to prevent the loss of billions of dollars in annual tax revenues and detect, disrupt, and dismantle terrorist financial support networks, the ATF conducts sophisticated investigations to identify the illicit trafficking of tobacco products. The availability of CBFT data could significantly enhance the ability of ATF agents, analysts, and investigators to identify entities suspected of engaging in interstate tobacco diversion operations through the identification and analysis of funds transmittals associated with the purchase or sale of illicit tobacco products.

4.4.4 Government Sanctions/Targeted Financial Measures

Agency	Type	Use Case Title
Office of Foreign Assets Control (OFAC)	Reactive	Narcotics Sanctions Investigations Pursuant to Executive Order 12978 and the Kingpin Act
Financial Crimes Enforcement Network (FinCEN)	Reactive	Special measures against entities of "Primary Money Laundering Concern" - USA PATRIOT Act Section 311 Analysis

Office of Foreign Assets Control (OFAC)

In its effort to support United States foreign policy and national security goals, the United States Department of the Treasury's Office of Foreign Assets Control (OFAC) works to administer and enforce economic and trade sanctions against targeted foreign countries, terrorists, international narcotics traffickers, and those engaged in activities related to the proliferation of weapons of mass destruction. OFAC seeks to achieve this mission by imposing controls on transactions and freezing foreign assets under United States jurisdiction.

Narcotics Sanctions Investigations Pursuant to Executive Order 12978 and the Kingpin Act

To combat the threat posed by international narcotics traffickers, the President of the United States may impose sanctions pursuant to Executive Order 12978 (Colombian drug cartels) or the Foreign Narcotics Kingpin Designation Act ("Kingpin Act").

The long-term effectiveness of Executive Order 12978 and the Kingpin Act is enhanced by the Office of Foreign Assets Control's authority to make derivative designations of foreign individuals and entities that are owned or controlled by or are materially assisting, financial supporting, or providing goods or services in support of the narcotics trafficking activities of designated narcotics traffickers.

Access to CBFT data could enhance the ability of OFAC sanctions investigators to make derivative designations. By cross-referencing identifying information contained in CBFT transactions with additional data resources, OFAC sanctions investigators could trace the flow of financial transactions between foreign narcotics traffickers and their support networks.

Financial Crimes Enforcement Network (FinCEN)
Special measures against entities of "Primary Money Laundering Concern" - USA PATRIOT Act Section 311 Analysis

The USA PATRIOT Act made a number of amendments to the BSA intended to facilitate the prevention, detection, and prosecution of money laundering and terrorist financing. Section 311 of the USA PATRIOT Act grants the Secretary of the Treasury authority, after finding that reasonable grounds exist for concluding that a foreign jurisdiction, institution, class of transactions, or type of account is of "primary money laundering concern," to require domestic financial institutions and domestic financial agencies to take certain "special measures" against the primary money laundering concern designed to increase information gathering or prohibit transactions with the designee.

Since 2002, the Department of the Treasury has strategically utilized the power of Section 311 to isolate rogue actors of primary money laundering concern that present significant risks to the integrity of both domestic and international financial systems. The analysis of CBFT transactions could enhance the ability of FinCEN analysts to evaluate the effectiveness of Section 311 actions. By examining key data elements contained in CBFT transactions, such as names, addresses, and account information, FinCEN analysts would be better able to monitor the flow of CBFT transactions to or from a designee of primary money laundering concern. Such analysis could improve FinCEN's analysis of the efficacy of Section 311 actions and help to ensure their effective implementation.

4.4.5 Tax Evasion

Agency	Type	Use Case Title
Internal Revenue Service Criminal Investigation (CI)	Reactive	Tax Evasion Investigations
Internal Revenue Service Small Business Self Employed (SB/SE)	Proactive	Offshore Tax Haven Abuse Investigations

Internal Revenue Service Criminal Investigation (CI)

In its effort to foster confidence in the tax system and compliance with the law, Internal Revenue Service Criminal Investigation (CI) investigates potential criminal violations of the Internal Revenue Code and related financial crimes.

Tax Evasion Investigations

Maintaining public confidence in the fairness of the tax system is vital to effective tax administration. In the United States, compliance with tax laws relies heavily on voluntary compliance. The overall compliance rate achieved under the United States revenue system is high. Nevertheless, an unacceptably large amount of the tax that should be paid every year is not, giving rise to the "tax gap." The gross tax gap was estimated to be $345 billion in 2001.[9] This noncompliance by taxpayers undermines public confidence and threatens the ability of the IRS to effectively administer our nation's tax system.

To help close the tax gap, CI special agents and analysts work to identify sophisticated schemes to defraud the government of tax revenue. The availability of CBFT data could significantly improve the efficiency of CI's investigations by allowing analysts to trace the flow of revenue from entities seeking to conceal income subject to taxation.

Internal Revenue Service Small Business Self Employed (SB/SE)

The mission of the IRS Small Business/Self-Employed (SB/SE) Division is to apply the tax law with integrity and fairness. The SB/SE Division works to achieve this mission by helping customers understand and comply with applicable tax laws. The SB/SE Division has developed several initiatives, such as the Abusive Tax Scheme Program, to help ensure compliance with these laws.

Offshore Tax Haven Abuse Investigations

The Abusive Tax Scheme Program was developed by the IRS to identify taxpayers who exploit the secrecy laws of offshore jurisdictions in an attempt to conceal income subject to tax in the United States. These jurisdictions are commonly referred to as "tax havens" because they offer financial secrecy and impose little or no tax on income from sources outside their jurisdiction. The exploitation of offshore tax havens by United States citizens has resulted in the loss of billions of dollars in tax revenue.

In an effort to address this loss of revenue, IRS SB/SE analysts seek to proactively identify taxpayers engaged in the exploitation of offshore tax havens. The availability of CBFT data would enhance the IRS's ability to identify taxpayers attempting to conceal income subject to taxation. By conducting geographic analysis of financial institution data contained in CBFT transactions, IRS SB/SE analysts could proactively identify taxpayers seeking to transmit taxable income from the United States to known offshore tax havens.

4.4.6 Individual Fraud

Agency	Type	Use Case Title
United States Secret Service (USSS)	Reactive	Identity Theft and Credit Card Fraud Investigations

---

[9] "Tax Year 2001 Federal Tax Gap," Internal Revenue Service, 14 February 2006, United States Department of the Treasury, Internal Revenue Service, 13 March 2008 <http://www.irs.gov/pub/irs-utl/taxgap021406.pdf >.

United States Secret Service (USSS)

In an effort to carry out its dual missions of protection and criminal investigations, the United States Secret Service works to both safeguard our nation's leaders and investigate financial crimes. The primary investigative mission of the Secret Service is to safeguard the payment and financial systems of the United States. The Secret Service accomplishes this mission through the enforcement of counterfeiting statutes designed to preserve the integrity of United States currency. To ensure the safety of our nation's financial systems, the Secret Service also investigates crimes involving electronic funds transmittals, credit card fraud, and identity theft.

Identity Theft and Credit Card Fraud Investigations

To combat identity theft and credit card fraud, Secret Service agents seek to detect financial transactions involving proceeds from the sale of identification and credit card data. The availability of CBFT transactions would enhance the efficiency of Secret Service agents investigating these crimes. By cross-referencing lead information with key data elements in CBFT transactions, such as name, account and telephone numbers, Secret Service agents would be able to more efficiently identify funds transmittal activity associated with the sale of identification and credit card data.

4.4.7 Market Stability and Oversight

Agency	Type	Use Case Title
United States Securities and Exchange Commission (SEC)	Reactive	Foreign Corrupt Practices Act Investigations
Financial Crimes Enforcement Network (FinCEN)	Proactive	Unregistered Money Services Businesses (MSBs) Identification
Financial Crimes Enforcement Network (FinCEN)	Proactive	Emerging High-Risk Financial Trend Identification

United States Securities and Exchange Commission (SEC)

In its effort to maintain the integrity of United States securities markets and protect the interests of investors, the Securities and Exchange Commission (SEC) works to maintain fair, orderly, and efficient markets and administer federal laws governing United States securities. The SEC works to promote fair and efficient markets through an effective and flexible regulatory environment. The SEC works to detect problems in the securities markets, prevent and deter violations of federal securities laws, and alert investors to possible wrongdoing.

Foreign Corrupt Practices Act Investigations

During SEC investigations in the 1970s, hundreds of United States companies admitted to making questionable or illicit payments to foreign government officials. Congress enacted the Foreign Corrupt Practices Act (FCPA) in 1977 to end the bribery of foreign officials and to restore public confidence in the integrity of the United States business system.

The availability of CBFT data could significantly improve the efficiency of SEC attorneys investigating violations of the FCPA. Through the analysis of key data elements in CBFT transactions, such as the names of the originator and beneficiary, SEC attorneys would be able to more effectively trace the flow of payments to persons or entities including foreign government officials, politicians, and political parties.

Financial Crimes Enforcement Network (FinCEN)
Unregistered Money Services Businesses (MSB) Identification

Certain MSBs must register with FinCEN under the BSA. In addition, MSBs are subject to the anti-money laundering program, reporting, and recordkeeping requirements of the BSA. Registration of MSBs helps ensure that these businesses operate within the formal financial system, and are subject to examination by the Internal Revenue Service and state government agencies.

MSBs that fail to comply with registration and other requirements of the BSA are vulnerable to exploitation by entities seeking to engage in terrorist financing, money laundering, and other illicit activity. Activities of MSBs operating in violation of BSA registration requirements may not be detected and examined for compliance with anti-money laundering program, reporting, and recordkeeping requirements. To combat such threats, FinCEN conducts proactive analysis to identify entities that may be operating as unregistered MSBs. The addition of CBFT data would significantly increase FinCEN's ability to identify these businesses. By analyzing CBFT transactions for high volume activity and cross-referencing originator information with additional data resources, FinCEN analysts would be better able to proactively identify entities operating as unregistered MSBs; ultimately enhancing FinCEN's efforts to safeguard the financial system from the abuses of financial crime.

Emerging High-Risk Financial Trend Identification

The Secretary of the Treasury has delegated overall authority for the enforcement of, and compliance with, the BSA to the Director of FinCEN. The Secretary has delegated BSA examination authority to federal regulators. To assist regulatory agencies with the examination of financial institutions, FinCEN conducts sophisticated analysis of BSA data to proactively identify emerging high-risk products, services, locations, and types of customers that may be exploited by entities seeking to engage in illicit financial activity.

Access to CBFT data would greatly enhance FinCEN's ability to identify high-risk financial areas through the analysis of systemic vulnerabilities or newly emerging trends in the cross-border transmittal of funds. By providing industry-wide assessments on high-risk products, services, locations, and types of customers to both the federal regulatory agencies and the financial industry, FinCEN could help improve regulatory efficiency of financial institution examinations and assist the financial industry in evaluating new lines of business while improving their risk-based approach to anti-money laundering.

4.5   Current Use of CBFT Data by Foreign Financial Intelligence Units

Since 1995, the United States has pursued a policy of promoting a worldwide network of FIUs in the fight against financial crimes and terrorist financing. FinCEN, as the FIU of the United States, is a member of the Egmont Group of FIUs. The Egmont Group is an international network of 108 jurisdictions that have implemented national centers to collect information on suspicious or unusual financial activity from the financial industry, to analyze the data, and to make it available to appropriate national authorities and other FIUs.

In order to demonstrate the value of the data collected in CBFT transactions with regard to financial crimes and terrorist financing, FinCEN contacted representatives from multiple international FIUs to identify their current use of cross-border funds transmittal data. During the interviews with each FIU, the agencies emphasized the significant value of CBFT data to their investigative missions, as well as the benefit to international cooperative efforts to fight financial crimes.

Representatives from the FIUs identified the following key benefits resulting from their agency's collection and analysis of CBFT transactions:

- The collection of CBFT transactions is critical in the fight against money laundering and terrorist financing as organized crime groups and terrorist financiers have increased operations in numerous jurisdictions across a global environment.

- Sharing of CBFT transactional data has enhanced international cooperation between FIUs and has resulted in the tracing of proceeds from transnational criminal activity and funds used in the financing of terrorism.

- Access to CBFT transactions has given investigators the ability to detect and disrupt the "layering" and "integration" stages of money laundering operations; stages often not detected through the analysis of traditional anti-money laundering reporting measures. Through the analysis of CBFT transactions and complementary data, such as intelligence contained in SARs and CTRs, investigators are able to detect illicit financial activity at multiple points in the money laundering lifecycle, including the placement, layering, and integration stages.[10]

Representatives from each of the FIUs emphasized the significant value of CBFT data to their current investigative missions as distinct from other reported data such as their equivalents of CTRs and SARs, as well as the benefit to global efforts to fight financial crimes. FIU representatives indicated that through the collection and analysis of CBFT data, FinCEN could

[10] The term "money laundering" is the criminal practice of processing ill-gotten gains, or "dirty" money, through a series of transactions; in this way the funds are "cleaned" so that they appear to be proceeds from legal activities. Money laundering generally does not involve currency at every stage of the laundering process. Although money laundering is a diverse and often complex process, it basically involves three independent steps that can occur simultaneously: placement, layering, and integration. The first and most vulnerable stage of laundering money is placement. The goal is to introduce the unlawful proceeds into the financial system without attracting the attention of financial institutions or law enforcement. Placement techniques include structuring currency deposits in amounts to evade reporting requirements or commingling currency deposits of legal and illegal enterprises. The second stage of the money laundering process is layering, which involves moving funds around the financial system, often in a complex series of transactions to create confusion and complicate the paper trail. The ultimate goal of the money laundering process is integration. Once the funds are in the financial system and insulated through the layering stage, the integration stage is used to create the appearance of legality through additional transactions. These transactions further shield the criminal from a recorded connection to the funds by providing a plausible explanation for the source of the funds.

enhance international cooperative efforts to fight financial crimes and improve the ability of FIUs throughout the world to safeguard the financial system from the abuse of money laundering, terrorist financing, and other illicit activity (see Appendix B.)

4.6 Data Usability, Quality, and Prototyping

4.6.1 Data Usability

Through the business use case interview process, law enforcement and regulatory agencies provided numerous examples of how they could utilize CBFT data to support a broad range of investigations. However, concerns remained about the data which are addressed below.

4.6.1.1 Sufficiency of existing CBFT data elements for investigative purposes

The study team also sought to identify the specific data elements in CBFT transactions that would be most useful to the investigative efforts of law enforcement and regulatory agencies. Agency representatives identified the following data elements as critical to their investigations:

- Name and address of the originator
- Name and address of the beneficiary
- Amount of the transmittal
- Execution date of the transmittal
- Account number
- Originator's financial institution
- Beneficiary's financial institution

Comparative analysis of these data elements with the data maintained by financial institutions under the current Funds Transfer Rule, and the data elements identified by law enforcement and regulatory agency representatives as critical, indicate that no new CBFT data elements would be needed to conduct the type of analysis illustrated in the business use cases, although the reporting of additional data fields would add value.

4.6.1.2 Necessity of historical CBFT data for investigative purposes

The study team also examined the volume of data necessary to conduct the types of analysis illustrated in the use cases. The study team determined that the use cases were not dependent on the availability of historical CBFT data and that only two use cases would require several months of data to begin analysis. During the interview process, agency representatives indicated that going forward, FinCEN's preliminary suggestion to maintain five years of CBFT data online and readily available, with another five years of archival data stored electronically, would be sufficient for their agencies to engage in the types of analyses illustrated in the use cases.

4.6.1.3 Sufficiency of existing recordkeeping threshold for investigative purposes

The study team also sought to determine how the current $3,000 record keeping threshold might affect the ability of law enforcement and regulatory agencies to perform the types of analyses detailed in their use cases. Each agency indicated that the basic information already obtained and maintained by United States financial institutions (banks and non-bank financial institutions) pursuant to the Funds Transfer Rule, including the $3,000 recordkeeping threshold would provide sufficient basis for meaningful data analysis. A majority of agencies, however, indicated that having access to cross border funds transmittals below the $3,000 threshold would improve their ability to detect and disrupt illicit financial activity. For example, law enforcement agency representatives indicated that financial transactions used to facilitate illicit activities, such as terrorist financing or human trafficking, frequently occur below the current $3,000 recordkeeping threshold, often at levels below $1,000. The ability of law enforcement and regulatory agency investigators to analyze CBFT transactions at these lower thresholds would enhance their ability to detect and disrupt the types of illicit activities described in the business use cases.

4.6.2 Data Quality

In order to examine the quality of information provided in cross border funds transmittal data, the study team undertook a detailed analysis of CBFT data samples provided by the financial industry. The analysis of these data samples sought to determine:

- the population frequency of key data elements identified by law enforcement and regulatory agencies as critical to their investigations

- the data quality level of key data elements necessary to conduct the type of analyses illustrated in the business use cases

In order to determine the population frequency of key data elements identified by law enforcement and regulatory agencies as critical to their investigations, the study team conducted analysis of CBFT data samples provided by the financial industry (see figures 4-3 and 4-4).

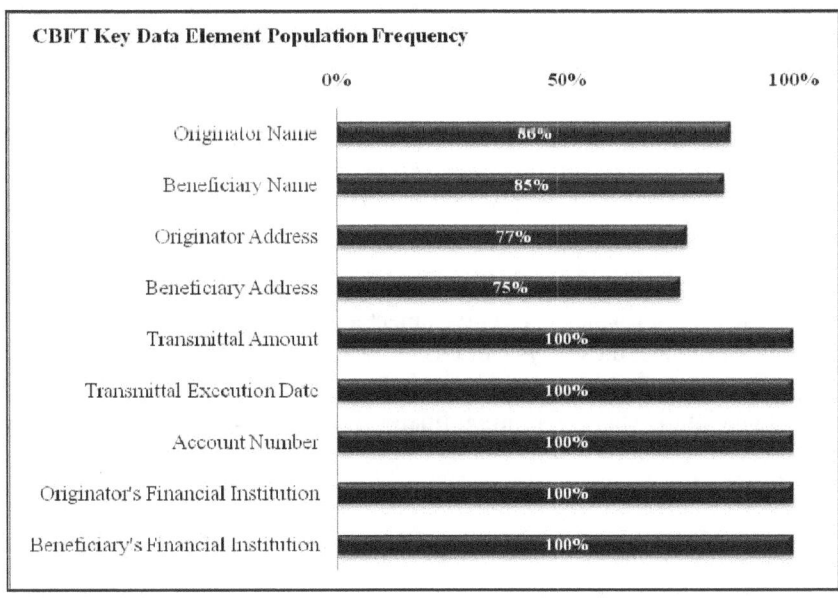

Figure 4-3 CBFT Key Data Element Population Frequency- Financial Institutions

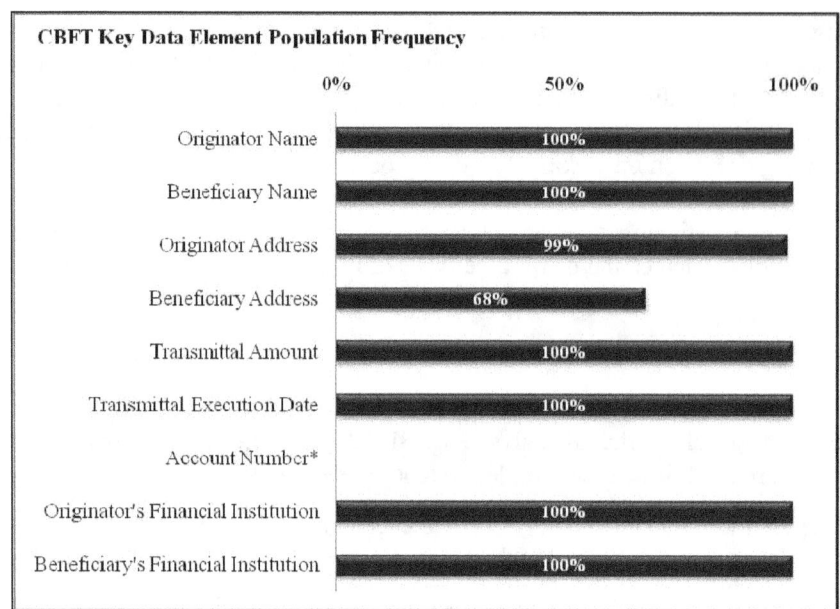

*Note: The study team was unable to provide population frequency statistics for the "Account Number" field for non-bank financial institutions since this field is not included in non-bank financial institution CBFT transactions.

Figure 4-4 CBFT Key Data Element Population Frequency- Non-Bank Financial Institutions

4.6.3   Data Prototyping

In order to determine if the data quality level of key data elements contained in the CBFT data samples was sufficient to conduct the types of analyses illustrated in the business use cases, FinCEN conducted prototyping analysis of the CBFT data. The study team developed several prototype examples demonstrating how CBFT data can be used to conduct the types of analysis identified in the business use cases. The following examples illustrate how CBFT data, when combined with additional data resources, enhance the ability of law enforcement and regulatory agencies to investigate entities suspected of engaging in illicit activity through the identification of new lead information including names, account numbers, and financial transactions.

In the first prototype, CBFT data was combined with additional data resources to develop a network of potentially illicit financial activity connected with a subject of interest to law enforcement. In this example, the analysis of CBFT data resulted in the identification of new lead information, including financial institution accounts, financial transactions, and previously unknown entities potentially engaged in illicit financial activity (see fig. 4-5).

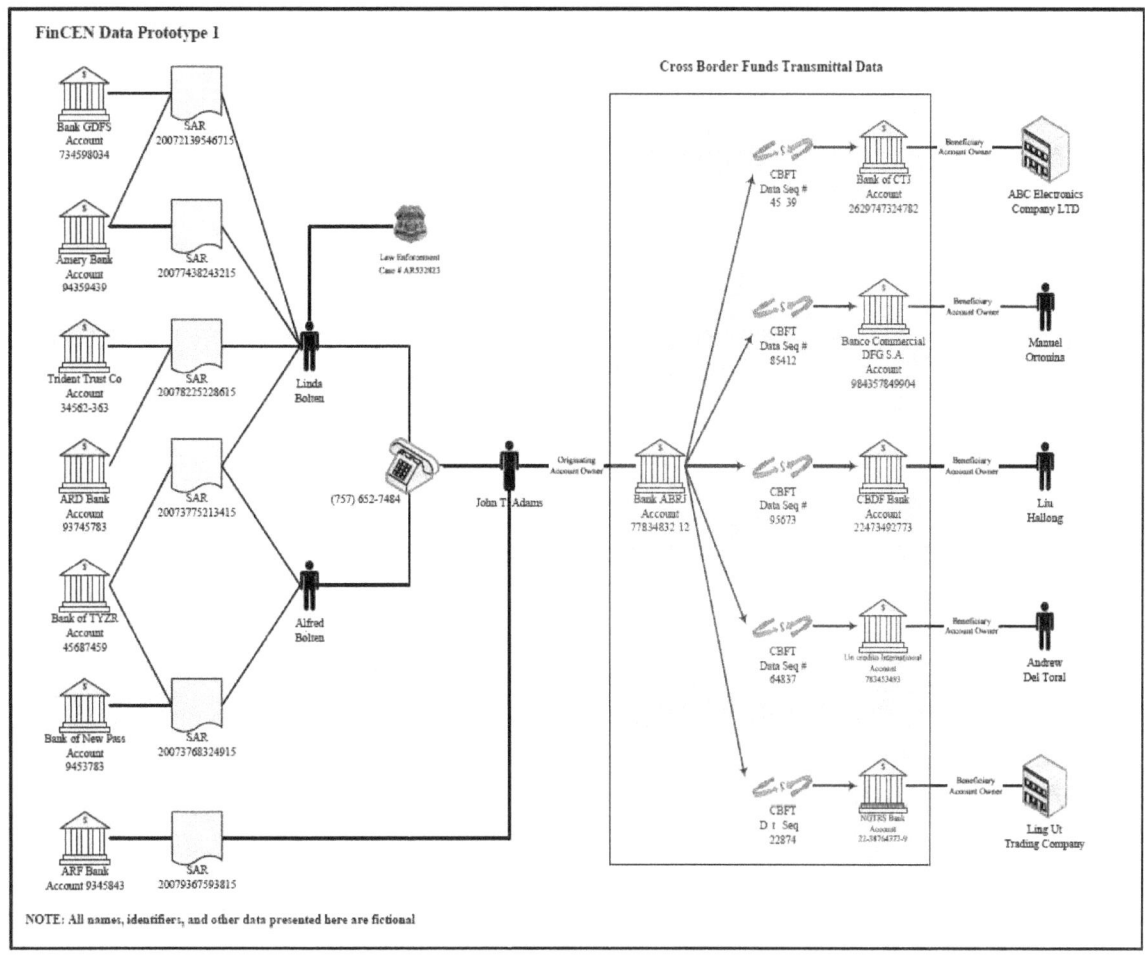

Figure 4-5 FinCEN Data Prototype 1

In the second prototype, the study team demonstrated the complementary potential value of CBFT data in relation to BSA filings such as Suspicious Activity Reports (SARs) and Currency Transaction Reports (CTRs). In this example, the analysis of CBFT originating and beneficiary account information allowed the analyst to connect two networks of potentially illicit financial activity previously thought to be unrelated. The connection of these networks resulted in the identification of new relationships between entities potentially engaged in illicit activity (see figure 4-6).

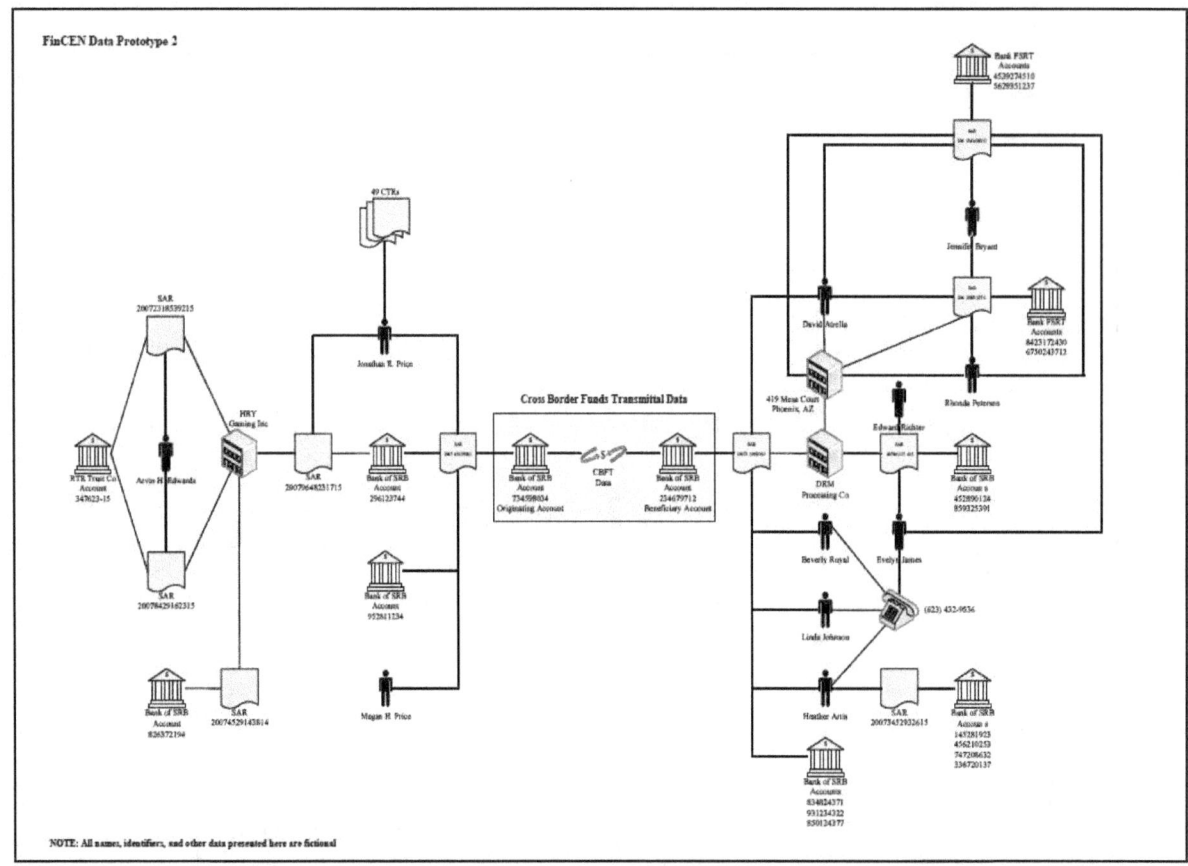

Figure 4-6 FinCEN Data Prototype 2

In order to further evaluate the quality of key data elements contained in the CBFT data, the study team cross-referenced a three-month sample of CBFT data with FinCEN's internal investigative indices. This cross-reference revealed hundreds of instances where key data elements contained in CBFT transactions, such as originator and beneficiary names and account numbers, were associated with cases contained in FinCEN's investigative indices and/or pointed to additional investigative leads. While the study team limited the analysis to a high-level review of these associations, however, their existence within on this relatively small data set highlights the potential value of CBFT data in the detection and disruption of illicit activity.

Through the analysis of CBFT data samples obtained from the financial industry, the study team determined that both the population frequency and quality of key CBFT data elements were sufficient to allow for meaningful analysis. Using the data prototyping examples, the study team was able to demonstrate the ability to conduct such analysis. Based on analysis and prototyping of the CBFT data samples, the study team determined that the access to CBFT transactions could enhance the ability of law enforcement and regulatory agencies to detect and disrupt the types of illicit activities described in the business use cases.

5. Implications to the Financial Industry

5.1 Survey Approach

To solicit input from the financial industry on the effects of a potential CBFT reporting requirement, FinCEN contracted with an experienced survey contractor, Claes Fornell International ("CFI"), through the Federal Consulting Group[11] to gather qualitative information and quantitative data from sectors of the industry that could be affected by the reporting requirement. FinCEN developed the survey content with significant input from the BSAAG CBFT subcommittee.

On behalf of FinCEN, CFI distributed the CBFT survey to 247 depository institutions and 32 money transmitters that conduct CBFT transactions on behalf of their own customers or that act as a correspondent bank for other financial institutions:

- "Depository institutions" were defined as depository institution members of the Society of Worldwide Interbank Financial Telecommunications (SWIFT) user group located or doing business in the United States, including offices or agents of non-U.S. chartered depository institutions.

- "Money transmitters" were defined as non-bank financial institutions that were registered with FinCEN as a money transmitter on November 10, 2007 and reported at least 20 branch location in the United States.

The survey questionnaire was designed to solicit input from financial institutions on the implementation and recurring costs and the likely effects on their operational activities of a potential CBFT reporting requirement. FinCEN conducted follow-up interviews with a selected number of survey respondents to explore their responses further.

CFI received responses from 81 financial institutions, which represented a 29% response rate. The CBFT survey and CFI's final report are included in Appendix C.

5.1.1 Potential CBFT Reporting Requirement as Defined for the Survey

Under a potential CBFT reporting requirement, based on existing recordkeeping obligations, a financial institution physically located or doing business within the United States would report to FinCEN a limited set of data elements from the SWIFT MT103 payment messages or transmittal orders that it directly sent to or received from a depository institution or non-bank financial institution (a money transmitter) physically located or doing business outside the United States.[12]

---

[11] The Federal Consulting Group (FCG), a federal government organization within the Department of the Treasury, is the executive agent for the American Customer Satisfaction Index (ACSI), the leading national indicator of customer satisfaction with U.S. products and services. The FCG and its partners, Claes Fornell International (CFI Group USA) and the Steven M. Ross School of Business at the University of Michigan, comprise the ACSI Team.

[12] For purposes of this study, FinCEN asked industry to consider a potential requirement to report only the following data elements from either a cross-border SWIFT MT103 funds transfer message (for depository institutions) or any cross-border electronic transmittal order (for money transmitters): 1) name and address of the originator or transmitter, 2) amount, 3) execution date, 4) name of the beneficiary's or recipient's bank, and 5) name, address, account number, or other beneficiary or recipient information (if available in the MT103 payment message). If a depository institution, the reporting U.S. institution would provide only this information, formatted in the original payment message's SWIFT MT103 format (for depository institutions) or other format as specified by FinCEN (for money transmitters), in a batch report once each business day to FinCEN. In addition, only messages valued at $3,000 or more would be reported. See Appendix C for the complete definition of the potential reporting requirement used by industry to develop their compliance cost estimates.

5.2   Survey Analysis

5.2.1   Reporting Volumes

Based upon the potential reporting requirement as described for the survey, the responding depository institutions indicated that they would need to report data on about one of every five of the electronic funds transfers they process within the United States. Further, these depository institutions indicated that including all cross-border electronic funds transmittals valued at less than $3,000 would increase the total to approximately one in every three electronic funds transfers processed in the United States and would therefore increase their costs of reporting.

The responding money transmitters indicated that they would need to report data on about one in every 100 of all the electronic funds transmittals they process within the United States. These money transmitters indicated, however, that including all cross-border electronic funds transmittals valued at less than $3,000 would significantly increase the total number reportable and therefore could significantly increase their costs.

5.2.2   Implementation and Annual Recurring Costs

Many survey respondents noted that while the level of change necessary to implement the potential reporting requirement, as described in the survey, could vary based on the specifics of a final reporting requirement, most respondents expected relatively minor changes to their systems and operations. However, a number of both large and foreign depository institutions, along with many small money transmitters, noted a relatively greater level of change to their current systems or other operational and compliance areas. Generally though, both depository institutions and money transmitters reported that the potential reporting requirement as described in the survey would, on average, slightly increase their costs of doing business.

The survey responses of the largest domestic depository institutions (over $1 billion in assets) that utilize SWIFT estimated an average of just under $250,000 for implementation costs and an annual recurring cost of just over $82,000. A large number of respondents, however, believed that the costs would be considerably less, as the median costs were just over $100,000 for implementation and approximately $35,000 for annual costs.

The average costs were considerably lower in the survey responses of foreign depository institutions that utilize SWIFT. The average implementation costs were estimated to be just over $52,000 and annual costs estimated at approximately $64,000. Median costs were considerably lower among foreign depository institutions with implementation estimated at about $40,000 and annual costs just over $20,000.

Average and median costs for those with unknown assets and assets of $1billion or less represented a small sample of respondents. Because only a small number of money transmitters responded to the survey, the study team was unable to obtain a comparable range for estimating the implementation and recurring costs. Appendix C provides a further breakdown of the costs as reported by each stratum.

The charts below show a breakdown of one-time implementation and annual costs for all depository institutions (i.e. domestic and U.S. branches of foreign SWIFT depository institutions). Software/development, systems upgrades and programming are estimated to account for nearly half of the implementation costs. Personnel and on-going management are estimated to account for two-thirds of the annual costs. [13]

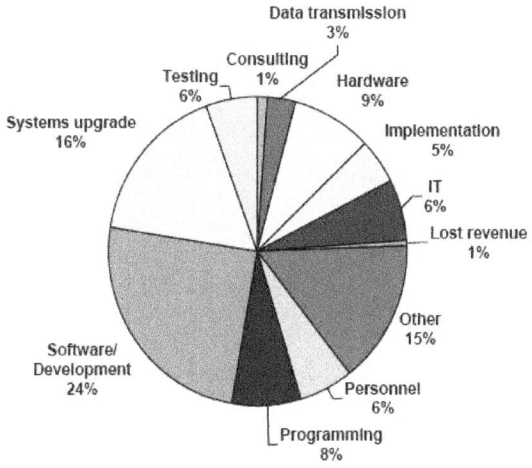

Figure 5-1 One-time implementation costs by source

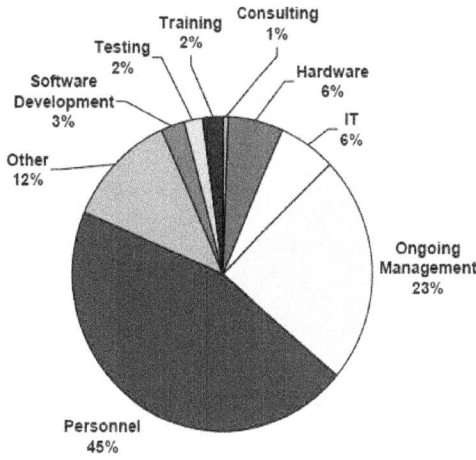

Figure 5-2 Annual costs by source

Survey respondents also expected an increase in the cost of complying with the new reporting requirement as compared to the current costs of complying with subpoenas or other legal demands under current recordkeeping requirements. Overall, nearly two-thirds of respondents thought that complying with the potential reporting rule would be more costly than responding to subpoenas.

---

[13] FinCEN 2008 Cross-Border Electronic Funds Transfer Survey, March 2008

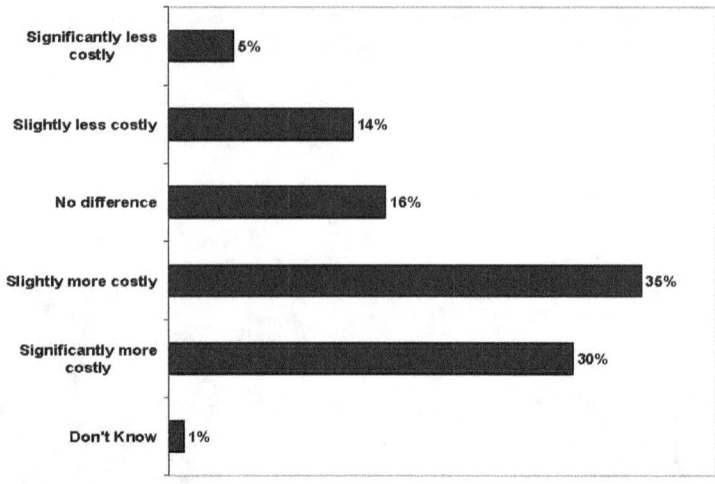

Figure 5-3 Expected effect on costs of complying compared to current subpoena and other legal costs under the recordkeeping requirement.

5.2.3 Impact on Operational Activities

Respondents indicated that implementation of a potential reporting requirement would have an effect upon different parts of their organizations, primarily affecting their operations, IT, compliance, as well as internal audit, legal and training areas. While many respondents believed that a potential reporting requirement would affect their costs, respondents generally did not believe that the volume, value or quality of transmittals would be adversely affected.

Nearly 60% of respondents thought there would be no change in volume; however 23% felt they would experience a slight/significant decrease. The majority of respondents (63%) felt there would be no change in the value of transmittals; however, 23% also felt there would be slight/significant decrease in value. More than two-thirds of respondents expected there to be no change in the quality of transmittals; less than 10% thought there would be a decrease in quality. U.S. branches of foreign depository institutions indicated that they would be most likely to see a decline in the volume and value of transfers they conduct.

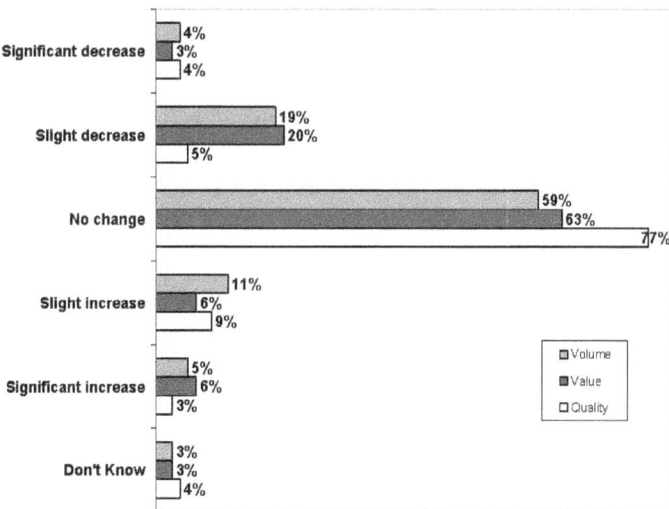

Figure 5-4 Requirements expected effect on volume, value and quality of transmittals

In follow-up interviews conducted with select financial institutions, many indicated that they use multiple internal systems to store funds transmittal data. The final specifications of a reporting requirement, should one be implemented, could be an additional cost factor if it requires a change to their current recordkeeping processes. Likewise, depending on the requirement of a reporting rule, data storage capacity may be an issue for some financial institutions who conduct a large volume of potentially reportable transactions.

5.2.4 Additional Feedback from Industry on the Implications of a Potential CBFT Reporting Requirement

Survey respondents were given an opportunity to provide additional input on several topics related to a potential CBFT reporting requirement. The study team identified several areas of importance to financial institutions.[14]

5.2.4.1 Alternative Reporting Methods or Implementation Approaches

Although many financial institutions (19 survey respondents) could not identify or did not offer recommendations for alternative reporting methods or implementation approaches, others did suggest methods or approaches that might potentially reduce the effect on financial institutions.

- Have FinCEN obtain CBFT information directly from the Society for Worldwide Interbank Financial Telecommunication (SWIFT) or some other centralized repository. (12 respondents)

---

[14] The following section summarizes the key points and issues that depository institutions and money transmitters raised in their responses to one of the survey's five open-ended questions. Because many institutions raised multiple points within their survey responses, the number of respondents associated with a given response will differ from the single primary response per respondent listing of issues in the report by CFI found in Appendix C.

- Report CBFT data less frequently than daily as described in the survey; most who responded suggested monthly reporting. (11 respondents)
- Have FinCEN provide a fully automated process for submitting reports, such as BSA e-filing, or provide the reporting software. (10 respondents)
- Leverage the current reporting capabilities by enhancing existing processes, such as the 314(a) or suspicious activity reporting processes. (7 respondents)
- Expand the reporting requirement to report all CBFT transactions rather than only those transactions that are currently required under the recordkeeping rule. (7 respondents)
- Reduce the scope of the reporting requirement through a risk-based approach or a higher dollar threshold. (6 respondents)
- Accept the data in the existing format used by financial institutions. (6 respondents)

5.2.4.2   Potential Unintended Consequences from a CBFT Reporting Requirement

Survey respondents were asked to identify any potential unintended consequences to their business resulting from a potential CBFT reporting requirement. While financial institutions were unable to quantify some of the potential unintended consequences, the study team did identify the following themes:

- The largest group of respondents indicated that they did not expect any potential unintended consequences as a result of a potential CBFT reporting requirement. (32 respondents)
- The next largest group of respondents noted that international CBFT business currently conducted in the United States could move away from the use of the U.S. dollar to another currency, increase the use of cover payments, or create other competitive disadvantages. (29 respondents)
- Customers may move to an alternative method for conducting transactions, such an informal fund transfer systems, which could reduce revenues for the financial institution. (12 respondents)
- Processing of fund transfers could be slowed, the overall efficiency of the U.S. payments system could be diminished, and costs to customers could increase. (12 respondents)
- Some customers who object to providing personal financial data to the U.S. government may structure payments to avoid a potential reporting requirement, which could lead to an increase in SAR filings. (5 respondents)
- Reporting CBFT data may result in an increase of subpoenas and requests for bank records and other customer information. (5 respondents)

5.2.4.3   Other Issues Raised by Industry to a CBFT Reporting Requirement

Financial institutions raised other concerns on a number of issues related to a potential reporting requirement in response to the survey and as part of the follow-up interviews, including:

- Customer's privacy concerns over providing personal and financial data to the U.S. government (especially customers located outside the United States).
- Data quality issues for financial institutions, including those that have international operations and must abide by privacy laws and regulations that vary from country to country which restrict the amount of data they may collect or keep.

- The ability of FinCEN to effectively manage a high volume of CBFT data, keep the information private and ensure that it is secure and properly disseminated to law enforcement.

- The true value and usability of CBFT data to law enforcement, the ability of law enforcement to effectively use a potentially significant volume of data.

- How regulators would use this data, including comparing it to the SARs and CTRs filed by the institution, and whether institutions would be cited for not identifying transactions that regulators feel should have been reported.

5.2.4.4 Outreach and Guidance Related to Implementation of a CBFT Reporting Requirement

When asked to identify what outreach or guidance FinCEN could provide either prior to or following the implementation of a CBFT reporting requirement, survey respondents indicated that the following would be most beneficial:

- Provide technical requirements and implementation guidance, clear and specific reporting definitions, and other related compliance expectations or advice. (36 respondents)

- Conduct webinars, seminars, and other training sessions that address both general and technical issues associated with the reporting requirement. (14 respondents)

- Publish frequently asked questions. (12 respondents)

- Establish a hotline for general and technical reporting questions. (8 respondents)

- Provide sufficient implementation lead time (as much as 12 to 18 months) and testing opportunities before requiring compliance with the reporting requirement. (8 respondents)

- Provide feedback from law enforcement on the value of CBFT data, including the number of investigations, arrests, fines, etc. associated with its use. (4 respondents)

5.3 Key Findings from the Survey

Key findings from the CBFT Survey of Financial Industry Entities include the following:

- Respondents expected an increase in the current cost of complying with the new reporting requirement as compared to costs under the current process of complying with subpoenas or other legal demands under current recordkeeping requirements.

- Respondents suggested many alternative reporting methods and implementation approaches to reduce the potential costs of a reporting requirement, such as reporting CBFT data weekly or monthly, having FinCEN obtain CBFT information directly from SWIFT or some other centralized repository, either expanding or further limiting which CBFT transactions would need to be reported, or accepting the data in the existing format used by financial institutions.

- Respondents consider customer privacy a significant concern.

- Respondents noted that the security and uses of CBFT data are also a significant concern, especially the ease of accessibility of the data to law enforcement.

- Respondents felt that outreach and guidance from FinCEN both before and after the implementation of a reporting requirement would be critical to its effective implementation.

6. Costs of Implementation

This section presents a rough order of magnitude (ROM) for the two potential operating models described in Section 3.3, Potential Operating Models for Disclosing CBFT Information:

- Standard Reporting Model – Each individual financial industry entity implements its own reporting systems and reports CBFT information to FinCEN.

- Hybrid Reporting Model – Financial institutions that are members of SWIFT direct it to report copies of CBFT information to FinCEN. Large MSBs report to FinCEN on their own behalf. Small and medium-size MSBs report to FinCEN using e-File capabilities provided by FinCEN rather than implementing their own reporting systems.

In order to develop the ROM for each of these potential operating models, the study team analyzed financial institution survey responses (see Section 5, Implications to the Financial Industry, and Appendix C, CFI Survey Results). Based upon this analysis, the study team identified three major categories of costs and, within each category, sub-categories of cost:

- Financial institution costs

  - Three industry sub-categories with different cost structures: depository institutions, large MSBs and medium/small MSBs

    - Two types of costs:

      - One-time costs to develop and implement a solution to report CBFT information

      - Recurring annual cost to operate/maintain the solution

- FinCEN costs

  - One-time costs to develop and implement a solution, built upon the foundation provided by the FinCEN modernized IT architecture, to receive, process, and disclose CBFT information

  - Recurring annual cost to operate/maintain the additional CBFT solution components

- Law enforcement agency costs

  - One-time costs to develop and implement a solution to receive CBFT information; the solution would be built upon existing channels to receive BSA data from FinCEN

  - Recurring annual cost to operate/maintain the additional CBFT solution components

To develop the ROM cost estimate, the study team identified for each of the two potential operating models, the key factors driving the one-time and recurring annual costs in each of the three categories and their subcategories of costs. Using these key cost driver factors, financial institution responses to the survey, and similar systems engineering efforts as a basis of estimation where industry-supplied data was not available, the study team developed ROM estimates for each of the potential operating models. ROMs were developed for the one-time and recurring annual costs for financial institutions, FinCEN and law enforcement agencies.

Table 7-1 presents the costs for the financial industry. It splits the depository institutions and MSB costs into their respective sub-categories. The table illustrates the average one-time implementation cost and the average recurring annual cost for each of the potential reporting models for depository institutions, MSBs, FinCEN, and law enforcement agencies.

Table 6-1					
		Standard Reporting Model		Hybrid Reporting Model	
Type	Size (Number of Anticipated Covered Institutions)	Average One-Time Implementation Cost	Average Recurring Annual Cost	Average One-Time Implementation Cost	Average Recurring Annual Cost
Depository Institutions	Large (5)	$249,787	$82,409	$0	$93,503
	Medium (92)	$249,787	$82,409	$0	$20,101
	Small (150)	$61,875	$59,526	$0	$6,753
MSBs	Large (6)	$250,006	$51,934	$250,006	$51,934
	Medium/Small (693)	$0	$60,000	$64	$395

Based on the results of their ROM cost analysis, the study team developed the following conclusions:

- The Hybrid Reporting Model significantly reduces the cost of a potential reporting requirement for depository institutions because the depository institutions would only incur annual reporting charges from SWIFT.

- The Hybrid Reporting Model significantly reduces the cost of a potential reporting requirement to MSBs, in aggregate, because the one-time and recurring annual costs of small/medium size MSBs using FinCEN's e-File data entry capabilities would be significantly less than the one-time and recurring annual costs of implementing/operating individual solutions. The costs to large MSBs would be the same under both models.

- The Hybrid Reporting Model slightly increases the costs of supporting a potential reporting requirement for FinCEN because of the higher implementation and maintenance/operation costs for the interface to SWIFT and the e-Filing CBFT data entry capabilities for small/medium size MSBs.

- Under both the Standard and Hybrid Reporting Models the cost to law enforcement agencies is the same.

7. Information Security and Privacy Controls

Implementation of either of the two potential operating models would improve CBFT information security and privacy controls over the existing operating model. Because no standards currently exist in the existing operating model, nearly a thousand financial institutions may disclose CBFT information to thousands of federal, state, and local law enforcement agencies with varying security and privacy controls across these different entities and agencies. In both of the two potential operating models, FinCEN, through its IT environment, would implement consistent security and privacy controls for receiving CBFT information from each financial industry entity and for providing access to CBFT information to each law enforcement agency it serves.

Appendix A, FinCEN IT Information Security and Privacy Controls, provides a more detailed description of the components of the FinCEN IT environment that provide security and privacy controls for BSA data.

7.1 FinCEN IT Environment Architecture Components Providing Security and Privacy Controls

The security and privacy control service capabilities in the FinCEN IT environment will be delivered through three primary architecture components – the Management and Support business application, portals, and database management systems.

The Management and Support business application will provide user identity management (e.g., characteristics of the user and information used to identify the user), user role management (e.g., what functions the user performs), and role-based business application access management (e.g., what business applications and data groups the user may access in his or her role).

The FinCEN IT environment will include three portals:

- The Public User Portal provides unregistered, public users controlled access to business applications and information secured for their use.

- The Registered User Portal provides registered users (e.g., BSA data filers in the financial industry, regulatory agencies, and law enforcement agencies) controlled access to business applications and data secured for their use.

- The Employee User Portal provides FinCEN employees and contractors and law enforcement personnel housed at FinCEN ("platformers") controlled access to business applications and data secured for their use.

These three portals will provide role-based access control to business applications. For example, if a law enforcement agency representative's role is to perform case-specific investigations on known subjects, then the portal would allow access to the basic (reactive) data analysis business application but not to the advanced (proactive) data analysis business application.

In addition to business application access control, the FinCEN IT environment database management systems will be capable of providing access control to BSA information at the data group level. For example, data groups could be established for Suspicious Activity Reports (SARs), Currency Transaction Reports (CTRs), and CBFTs. This will provide the ability for the data access level of each of these BSA data groups to be matched to the access privilege level of the internal or external user requesting the information. Thus, if a regulator or law enforcement representative is not authorized to perform basic (reactive) data analysis on CBFT data but is allowed to access CTR data, the BSA data access controls will ensure that only CTR data is returned by the basic (reactive) data analysis business application to the user.

7.2 FinCEN IT Environment Processes Providing Security and Privacy Controls

The FinCEN IT environment will have three primary BSA information security and privacy control processes – BSA Data Memoranda of Understanding (MOU), data access logging, and data access onsite inspections.

Only those regulatory and law enforcement agencies who have demonstrated a need for access to BSA data will be granted access. As a pre-requisite to receiving access to FinCEN systems or receive bulk data dissemination, there must be a signed MOU between FinCEN and the requesting agency. The MOU states the terms under which the agency participates in the program that FinCEN maintains to permit qualifying organizations to obtain direct electronic access to BSA information. The MOU covers a number of requirements to protect the security and privacy of BSA information, including limiting searches of BSA data and re-dissemination of BSA data, maintaining and providing information on BSA data inquiries, allowing inspections, preparing agency personnel for data access, and supplying FinCEN with information about authorized personnel.

In conjunction with the MOU, FinCEN provides the agency a BSA Information Access Security Plan that contains descriptions of the personnel, physical and computer security features required to ensure that BSA information is safeguarded appropriately by the agency and their authorized agency personnel.

FinCEN also requires each authorized agency personnel to sign, annually, a BSA Information Access User Acknowledgment. This document confirms that the authorized agency personnel understand and agree to the personnel, physical, and computer security features required to ensure that BSA information is safeguarded appropriately.

Within the FinCEN IT environment, internal and external users accessing BSA data through FinCEN business applications will have their data access logged. Similarly, regulatory and law enforcement agencies receiving BSA data through bulk dissemination will have to provide back to FinCEN audit logs on the access to the BSA data they received from FinCEN. These BSA data access audit logs will be used by FinCEN security and privacy personnel to determine if illicit activity occurred in the use of BSA data.

Based on the MOU and the analysis of BSA data access audit logs, FinCEN personnel will conduct periodic BSA data access inspections onsite at the regulatory and law enforcement agencies that have access to FinCEN business applications and/or receive bulk data from FinCEN. The purpose of the onsite inspection is to ensure that the technology and physical environment, security and privacy procedures and training, and personnel with access to BSA information all meet FinCEN's standards for security and privacy controls.

Should a potential illicit use of BSA data be detected, FinCEN will work with the agency personnel's management to investigate the incident and take action if necessary. If deemed necessary, FinCEN may pursue criminal and civil penalties against agency personnel or any other individual offender.

Appendix A: FinCEN IT Information Security and Privacy Controls

A.1 BSA Data Memoranda of Understanding (MOU)

Only those regulatory and law enforcement agencies who have demonstrated a need for access to BSA data will be granted access. As a pre-requisite to receiving access to BSA data, there must be a signed Memorandum of Understanding (MOU) between FinCEN and the agency.

The MOU states the terms under which the agency participates in the program that FinCEN maintains to permit qualifying organizations to obtain direct electronic access to BSA information. The MOU covers a number of requirements to protect the security and privacy of BSA information including:

- Limiting searches of BSA data – instructs agency personnel to limit the BSA information they obtain through a query to that BSA information which is immediately useful in connection with the specific matter prompting the query, use as much information as is reasonably available in framing and narrowing any query, maintain only that BSA information which is of value in connection with the specific matter prompting the query, and promptly destroy all documents or summaries obtained or generated through the query that is not of value for the specific matter queried.

- Limiting re-dissemination of BSA data – restricts the agency's dissemination of BSA data and case-related information and statistical or other information referencing or revealing BSA information.

- Maintaining and providing information on BSA data inquiries – instructs the agency to maintain records of relevant data files searched, retrieved, or both, and the purpose of the inquiry by agency personnel, and to supply FinCEN with information on the status or results of cases in which inquiries are made, any dissemination of BSA information, and other information such as statistical information about the agency's use of BSA information.

- Allowing inspections – informs the agency that FinCEN may arrange for the conduct of onsite and/or electronic inspections of the agency's electronic retrieval of information.

- Preparing agency personnel – instructs agency personnel they must have been the subject of a satisfactory background investigation completed in accordance with their agency's policies and receive training by FinCEN concerning the use of data analysis systems, the data files containing BSA information, and compliance with the terms of the MOU.

- Supplying authorized personnel information – instructs the agency to supply FinCEN with the names and identifying information of all authorized agency personnel for the purposes of controlling and monitoring access to BSA information and observance of the terms of the MOU.

In conjunction with the MOU, FinCEN provides the agency a BSA Information Access Security Plan which contains descriptions of the personnel, physical and computer security features required to ensure that BSA information is safeguarded appropriately by the agency and their authorized agency personnel.

FinCEN also requires each authorized agency personnel to sign on an annual basis a Bank Secrecy Act Information Access User Acknowledgment. This document confirms the authorized agency personnel understand and agree to the personnel, physical and computer security features required to ensure that BSA information is safeguarded appropriately.

A.2 BSA Business Application Access Controls

In Section 8.1, IT capabilities, and architecture components were defined that support improved application access control through the use of three portals – the Public User Portal (PUP), Registered User Portal (RUP), and Employee User Portal (EUP) – and role-based access controls. These portals provide a web site through which each of these three categories of users can access the modernized FinCEN IT environment.

For the PUP, the external user does not have to pre-register before gaining access to applications and information. Because of this, the PUP allows access to only those applications and information that FinCEN has deemed appropriate for unregistered public use. Examples of this are news releases, information on the FinCEN organization, and registration information. The PUP also provides appropriate firewalls and intrusion detection between the outside and FinCEN's IT environment.

The RUP provides the ability for an external user to register with FinCEN and receive access to those applications appropriate for their role. For example, a financial industry entity representative would have to register with FinCEN before receiving access to the e-File on-line data entry screen used to submit a BSA report. Similarly, a regulatory or law enforcement agency representative would have to register with FinCEN before receiving access to the basic (reactive) data analysis capability. Once FinCEN has confirmed the identity and appropriate role for the external user, the user will be established in the FinCEN security services application with business application access privileges appropriate for their role. The RUP will also provide appropriate firewalls and intrusion detection between the outside and FinCEN's IT environment and application access audit logs for analysis of user activity.

The EUP is similar to the RUP in its functions, except that FinCEN internal users (employees, contractors and law enforcement personnel housed at FinCEN) must undergo more extensive background checks before being established in the security services application and receiving business application access privileges appropriate for their role. Because the EUP is within FinCEN's secure IT environment, the EUP does not contain the extensive firewalls and intrusion detection needed for the RUP.

A.3 BSA Data Access Controls

Once an external or internal user has been cleared through the RUP or EUP, and their identity and role have been validated, the FinCEN business applications use the identity and role information to control access to BSA data groups.

Within the FinCEN IT environment, data group access controls will be established for different types of BSA data. For example, data groups could be established for Suspicious Activity Reports (SARs), Currency Transaction Reports (CTRs) and CBFTs. This will provide the ability for the data access level of each of these BSA data groups to be matched to the access privilege level of the internal or external user requesting the information. For example, if a regulator or law enforcement representative is not authorized to perform basic (reactive) data analysis on CBFT data, but is allowed to access CTR data, the BSA data access controls will ensure that only CTR data is returned by the basic (reactive) data analysis business application to the user.

Using these same BSA data access control services, FinCEN will control which BSA data regulatory and law enforcement agencies receive through bulk data dissemination business applications.

A.4 BSA Data Access Audit Logs

Within the modernized FinCEN IT environment, internal and external users accessing BSA data through FinCEN business applications will have their data access logged. Similarly, regulatory and law enforcement agencies receiving BSA data through bulk dissemination will have to provide back to FinCEN audit logs on the access to the BSA data they received from FinCEN.

These BSA data access audit logs will be used by FinCEN security/privacy personnel to determine if illicit activity occurred in the use of BSA data. The BSA data access audit logs will contain information on the user, the case/exam justifying the query, and the query they performed on the BSA data. The same advanced data analysis capabilities used to find patterns and trends in BSA data will be used to find patterns and trends in the queries of the BSA data performed by internal and external users.

Should a potential prohibited use of BSA data be detected, FinCEN will work with the user's management to investigate the incident and take action if necessary. If deemed necessary, FinCEN may pursue criminal and civil penalties against agency personnel or any other individual offender.

A.5 BSA Data Access Inspections

Based on the MOU and the analysis of BSA data access audit logs, FinCEN personnel will conduct periodic BSA data access inspections onsite at the regulatory and law enforcement agencies who have access to FinCEN business applications and/or receive bulk data from FinCEN. The purpose of the onsite inspection is to ensure that the technology and physical environment, security/privacy procedures and training, and authorized personnel all meet FinCEN's standards for security and privacy control.

Should a potential prohibited use of BSA data be detected, FinCEN will work with the agency personnel's management to investigate the incident and take action if necessary. If deemed necessary, FinCEN may pursue criminal and civil penalties against agency personnel or any other individual offender.

Appendix B: Financial Intelligence Unit Letters of Support

(Facsimiles of these letters appear on the following pages)

Australian Government

Australian Transaction Reports and Analysis Centre

OFFICE OF THE CHIEF EXECUTIVE OFFICER

Ref NJJ

15 February 2008

Mr James H Freis, Jr
Director
Financial Crimes Enforcement Network
United States Department of the Treasury
Post Office Box 39
Vienna Virginia 22183
USA

Dear Mr Freis

Re: International Wire Transfers

I refer to my previous discussions with Eric Nguyen and Andrew Shankman regarding this matter.

It is my understanding that the Financial Crimes Enforcement Network ("FinCEN") study on the capture of international wire transfers/cross border wire transfers recognises that the reporting of international wire transfers are both technically feasible for the US Government to adopt, and a valuable tool in your Government's ongoing efforts to combat money laundering ("ML") and terrorist financing ("TF"). Eric and Andrew indicated to me that FinCEN is currently preparing submissions to the US Treasury which include FinCEN's "inclusive and incremental approach"[1] to resolving outstanding technical and policy issues regarding the mandatory reporting of cross-border wire transfers.

The purpose of this letter and its attachments is to alert you to the Australian Government's long-held view of the significant value of the reporting of international wire transfers to AUSTRAC, not only in terms of our domestic law enforcement and revenue matters, but also in facilitating international cooperation in following the money trail associated with transnational and organised crime, and terrorism financing.

The value of this data is confirmed from AUSTRAC's extensive experience over 16 years in collating and disseminating such information, both domestically and internationally. AUSTRAC can see where the money goes overseas, and from where it comes, but international cooperation in tracking the funds of criminals is severely hampered because very few other countries have adequately considered the value of the collection of this information for domestic and international investigations. It is hoped that the USA will see this value and others will follow the USA lead, resulting in the identification and prosecution of the most significant criminals, who move their funds around the world.

---

[1] FinCEN Media Release dated 17 January 2007.

Although I will elaborate on this in more detail later it must be said at the outset that from an "Intelligence perspective", AUSTRAC's FIU strongly considers international wire transfers a critical component of its financial analysis and intelligence operations. Indeed, international wire transfer reports provide a comprehensive understanding of the *total* suspect financial activity. This means the collection of reports such as threshold deposit and withdrawal transactions, which only provide the FIU with details of the ML *'placement activity'* in most cases, can be linked to the wire transfers reports to gain a complete understanding of the entities and networks linked to the ML activity. Organised crime groups increasingly operate in numerous jurisdictions across a global environment, and the collection of international wire transfer reports' information becomes an integral component of the FIU's analysis in order to fully understand and detect ML activity. The collection of international wire transfer by an FIU enables it to 'join the dots', and detect the *layering and integration* stages of ML often linked to the placement activity.

In ML cases linked to tax evasion using tax haven jurisdictions, or drug importations or trade based money laundering matters, the financial activity will normally encompass deposit and withdrawal activity followed by wire transfers to overseas jurisdictions as part of a *layering and integration* processes whereby the funds are moved offshore in a round robin transaction scenario only to return if some other shape or form. In the case of drugs, the funds may simply be sent offshore to pay for the illicit drugs following the placement stages. In both of these examples, collection of the international wire transfer information is the only method available and *most* critical to the FIU in being able gain a full picture and understanding of the financial activity as part of its analysis.

AUSTRAC's Role

As Australia's Financial Intelligence Unit (FIU), AUSTRAC collects, analyses, and disseminates financial intelligence to 34 law enforcement, national security, revenue and social justice agencies, and to 49 overseas FIUs. This financial intelligence comes from the reporting to AUSTRAC of a range of financial transaction reports from the financial sector and non-banking financial sectors. Those reports include suspicious transaction reports, referred to as SUSTRs in Australia and which are similar to suspicious activity reports (SARs) in the US. We also collect cross border significant cash reports (ICTRs), and significant cash reports (SCTRs). Most importantly, we also capture all customer-based international wire transfers into and out of Australia, which we refer to as international funds transfer instructions (IFTIs). In our experience, the mandatory reporting of international wire transfers has provided AUSTRAC and our partner agencies with a vital and rich source of intelligence which has been instrumental in instigating, contributing and leading to the prosecution of individuals and organisations for many and varied serious crimes, both in Australia and overseas.

History

Australia first introduced mandatory reporting of international wire transfers in 1992 after a report by the Australian Government in 1991 on capital flight from Australia was linked to tax evasion. The report noted that international wire transfers were the most common way in which funds were channelled from Australia, and that the then current cash transactions monitoring system did not detect or monitor such transfers. The report recommended the mandatory reporting of *all* international wire transfers to AUSTRAC to assist in tracking money being wired to or from overseas, to assist investigations of offences of Australian laws, and cooperation in overseas investigations.

Two decisive factors which led to the collection of that data was that the data was already in electronic form, and the reporting entities advised that the cost would be minimised because of its electronic format, and if there was no threshold requirement. In fact, the reporting entities indicated that the cost would be significantly less than the programs for reporting of SARs and significant cash transactions.

In contrast, a transaction reporting threshold would have required the technical development of systems by each reporting entity, and also extensive staff training concerning the threshold levels. The response to these issues in Australia was a low cost technological solution developed and provided by AUSTRAC to reporting entities which was virtually seamless to their daily business, and required very little cost on their part. As it merely duplicated and then extracted the data from the technology systems of the reporting entities, there was no need for staff training. A bonus of the system was that international wire transfers were reported in real-time. These vital considerations enabled a quick and successful implementation of international wire transfer reporting requirements at very little cost to government or reporting entities.

Legislation

Legislative requirements regarding international wire transfers are contained in sections 3, and 17B to 17F of the *Financial Transactions Reports Act 1988* (FTR Act). Further prescribed details in relation to international wire transfers are contained in regulation IIAA of the *Financial Transaction Reporting Regulations 1990.*

In essence the FTR Act requires "cash dealers" in Australia to report international wire transfers for monies being telegraphically transferred or wired into or out of Australia. International wire transfers are reportable for *any amount,* whether paid for by cash or otherwise. It is only the reporting entity at the initial point of receipt of the international wire transfers in Australia, or at the point of the transmission from Australia who is required to report the international wire transfers. The maximum penalty for a person failing to submit an international wire transfer to AUSTRAC is imprisonment for up to two years[2]

These requirements have been included, and strengthened in the *Anti-Money Laundering and Counter-Terrorism Financing Act 2006.*[3] (AML/CTF Act) which will supersede the FTR Act provisions in December 2008.

The FIU

AUSTRAC now receives 16 million financial transaction reports ("FTR") per year[4], a very high volume of data compared with many FIUs around the world. This is due to the mandatory reporting of international wire transfers, in addition to the much smaller volumes of reports of suspicious activities, significant cash transactions and cross-border currency movements.

---

[2] Section 28(4) of the FTR Act.

[3] The AML/CTF Act came into effect on 13 December 2006, and was introduced to ensure that money laundering and terrorism financing risk in Australia is identified, managed and mitigated. As a result of the staggered implementation dates of the AML/CTF Act, the provisions relating to international wire transfers do not commence until 12 December 2008, and the FTR Act provisions continue in force until that time. For further details regarding the AML/CTF Act please refer to AUSTRAC's website www.austrac.gov.au.

[4] See page 33 of the AUSTRAC Annual Report 2006-7 (Report). For that year 15,740,744 financial transaction reports were received, at approximately 60,500 per day.

Importantly volume is not an issue as technology solutions are readily available to capture much larger volumes of data than these, and at relatively little cost. The volume is also important in AUSTRAC's analytical work, as our data mining tools are more effective on larger volumes of data. The AUSTRAC database currently contains about 90 million transaction reports. Although the volume of international wire transfers collected in Australia is significantly lower than the potential number of reports in the US, this should not be a deterrent to the capture of *all* wire transfers by FinCEN. As indicated, technology solutions to capture those volumes are readily available at relatively low cost.

More than 99.7 percent[5] of reports of financial transactions are submitted to AUSTRAC via the AUSTRAC developed secure reporting system, "EDDSWeb"[6]. Moreover, it is AUSTRAC policy where the volume of reports exceeds 250 per year, a reporting entity *must* report electronically. This method ensures higher levels of quality and timeliness of reports, and allows fast and accurate correction of data quality issues, as reports may be returned to reporting entities for correction via EDDSWeb.

EDDSWeb was developed by, and is fully maintained by AUSTRAC. This software captures the SWIFT format, and similar formats, so little work is needed by the reporting entities to use this software for reporting.

For smaller entities, such as alternative remittance services, AUSTRAC accepts international wire transfers via a batch file transfer format which requires the reporting entities to implement their own systems for converting the non-SWIFT data to the proper format prior to submitting the reports to AUSTRAC. AUSTRAC requires mandatory data fields that must be included in the international wire transfers report. Reporting entities can report by batch file, and single report via a web-faced interface operated by AUSTRAC. The interface enables institutions to upload prepared files automatically, and provides an interface for the manual upload of prepared batch files, and a form for extremely low volume reporting institutions to submit data. AUSTRAC has also developed, and distributes to financial institutions, a Microsoft Excel macro that can convert certain electronic data to the AUSTRAC systems.

In Australia, the largest four banks account for approximately 80 % of the reports of international wire transfers, with a second group of approximately 20 financial institutions comprising the majority of reporting institutions, and a large number of smaller entities reporting very small volumes. The cost to all, including AUSTRAC, is minimal.

Reports Received at AUSTRAC since 2001

The quantity of financial transaction reports received by AUSTRAC continues to increase significantly. As noted above, the database currently comprises about 90 million reports. Notably, international wire transfers provide the largest volume of financial transaction reports received with more than 50 million reports received over the past 5 years.

For the year 2006-07, a total of 13,017,467 international wire transfers were received[7], a 14 % increase from 2005. Figures for international wire transfers and other financial transaction reports are listed in the following table.

---

[5] Report at page 40.

[6] EDDSWeb is the acronym for Electronic Data Delivery Service.

[7] See page 36 of the Report.

Type of Report	2002-03	2003-04	2004-05	2005-06	2006-07
SARs	8,054	11,484	17,212	24,801	24,440
Significant cash	1, 979,446	2,056,617	2,288,373	2,416,427	2,675,050
Cross border cash	28,274	25,579	26,172	27,755	23,351
International wire transfers	7,493,765	8,685,843	10,243,774	11,411,961	13,017,467
Total Reports	9,509,539	10,779,523	12,575, 531	13,880,994	15,747,744[8]

Advantages

AUSTRAC has been capturing international wire transfers now for 16 years. What AUSTRAC can categorically say is that Australian law enforcement, national security and revenue programs have benefitted *greatly* from the capture of international wire transfers, as have a number of agencies in other countries through our law enforcement and FIU cooperation programs.

The value of the international wire transfer data, and its linkages in the AUSTRAC database to all of the other report types, can be found in the following table with more than 9 million searches on the database over the past 5 years by approximately 2,500 AUSTRAC and specified personnel from the law enforcement, national security, revenue and social justice agencies. It has assisted in more than 10,000 investigations, and provided tax revenue, directly derived from intelligence from the data, of more than $400 million. Most of these investigations and the revenue results involved intelligence from international wire transfers.

Database Searches	873,815	1,225,388	2,063,869	2, 546,372	2,348,363
Investigations	1,544	1,743	2,224	1,582	1,529
Taxation Revenue	AUD 99 million	AUD 72 million	AUD 62 million	AUD 91 million	AUD 87 million

Some of the advantages of the collection, analysis and dissemination of international wire transfer information are:

- International wire transfers are attractive to businesses because the service is a secure, quick and trusted means by which to send funds overseas. As international wire transfers do not involve the actual movement of currency, they are a rapid, reliable and secure method for transferring funds without the risks associated with moving physical currency. For the same reasons that apply to legitimate businesses, they are also

---

[8] There were 589,528 name searches undertaken by partner agencies.

attractive to criminals. The huge volumes of international wire transfers moving around the world daily, and the ability to indicate some legitimacy to the transactions through the financial sector, assist the criminals in layering and integrating their illicit funds, and those funds being transmitted for illegitimate purposes such as for terrorism financing. Data mining processes applied to this data when captured in one location can readily identify these criminals in the extensive amount of data.

- Terrorism is often financed by the movement of low value sums from participants in various countries. For example, reports on the 9/11 bombings in the US have indicated that as little as $500,000 was used to finance the attacks and that the money arrived in the US in numerous small value wire transfers from other countries. These transfers rang no alarm bells and were not identified until after US authorities began their investigations. The collection of all value international wire transfers and application of appropriate data mining techniques may have uncovered some of these transactions prior to the events of 9/11.

- The linking of other types of financial transaction reports to international wire transfer reports in a single database provides significant benefits in indentifying criminal activity. For example, a SAR which has been reported by a financial institution may not be enough in itself to alert law enforcement authorities about a criminal act. However, linking of that SAR to other report types, and in particular, to international wire transfers may provide a clearer picture of what may be occurring and the individuals and countries involved. International wire transfers may highlight the layering stage of money laundering which is not always apparent in other report types.

- International wire transfers provide a vital source of intelligence to law enforcement because of:
    - the ease of capture;
    - data they contain; and
    - the quantity of such transfers sent around the world on a daily basis.

- Through the use of data mining technologies, large volumes of international wire transfers provide the FIU with a greater ability to detect patterns of criminal behaviour and low value transactions which may have been overlooked.

- The use of international wire transfers in Australia, has been very successful in identifying numerous criminals not previously known to law enforcement agencies and has assisted greatly in intelligence led policing (see Attachment A).

- International wire transfers not only increase the extent of intelligence available to law enforcement agencies, but also enable the enhanced exchanges of vital intelligence between FIUs worldwide. Some type of international wire transfers reportage occurs in Argentina, Brazil, Canada, the Cook Islands, Ireland, Russia, South Africa, Switzerland, and the Netherlands.

- The Financial Action Task Force on money laundering (FATF) in its 40 + 9 Recommendations has addressed the issue of international wire transfers, although to a very limited degree in Special Recommendation VII suggesting that "financial institutions, including money remitters, should conduct enhanced scrutiny of and monitor for suspicious activity funds transfers which do not contain complete originator information" such as name, address and account number. In addition, FATF Recommendation 19 states: "Countries should consider the feasibility and utility of a system where banks and other financial institutions and intermediaries would report all domestic and international currency transactions above a fixed amount, to a national central agency with a computerised data base, available to competent authorities for use in money laundering or terrorist financing cases, subject to strict safeguards to ensure proper use of the information."

In both cases, the FATF has not gone far enough in addressing this issue. These solutions are useful, but only provide for records to be maintained and only assist law enforcement after the crime has been detected, the criminals have been identified by law enforcement and the location of each transaction has been identified by some other means. Very few criminals and very few of their transactions can be located merely through the collection of information in this way. Law enforcement will not know with which reporting entity the information is held and when and what transactions have occurred. When they eventually get that information, if they do, the money will likely have been dispersed globally and not be locatable. Reporting at the time of the transfer significantly enhances the ability of the law enforcement agencies to follow and intercept the funds.

- An addendum to the FATF requirements is that AUSTRAC, rather than the reporting entities, can ensure that Australian and overseas entities are including the required "originator information" in all international wire transfers into and out of Australia. As AUSTRAC has all of the reports of international wire transfers into and out of Australia, simple software analysis can indicate whether the information is in the international wire transfer. If it is not being included, AUSTRAC can provide advice to the reporting entities that it is not being included by them or their "correspondents" overseas, and the reporting entities can take steps to ensure it is included. If the failure to include the information in international wire transfers continues, the FATF can be alerted to that fact and appropriate follow up can be pursued by the FATF members.

- Costs for reporting of international wire transfers would be minimal to industry and FinCEN. Banks and non-bank financial institutions already have this information in an electronic format. The cost to AUSTRAC is minimal given the quality of information available, and the benefits it provides to investigating agencies and their results, together with benefits to international law enforcement. For example, AUSTRAC's FIU's direct costs are approximately AUD 7 million per year. International relations and intelligence capability costs are an additional AUD 2 million per year. The intellectual technology component comprises an estimated AUD 5 million.[9] Costs to set up access to the data in partner agencies, for approximately 2400 users, would include the cost of the computer/software connection and training at approximately AUD5 million. Leasing and administrative costs would amount to a further AUD5 million.

---

[9] It should be noted that all directorates within AUSTRAC utilise this service.

- The positive results for Australian law enforcement have been significant. AUSTRAC information contributed to the Australian Taxation Office assessments in 2006-7 of AUD 87 million alone.[10] In 2004-05, AUSTRAC international wire transfer information assisted law enforcement agencies to identify drugs to the street value of more than AUD 1 billion, stopping those drugs from coming into Australia and being sold on Australian streets, and consequently stopping the laundering of that amount of funds in Australia, much of which would have been sent off-shore. As international wire transfers are kept for a minimum of 8 years by AUSTRAC, it is a resource which can be utilised in an investigation at *any* stage.

- As the information is only captured when it is in Australia, that is the last point before it leaves Australia or the first point once it has entered Australia, concerns as to ownership of the information, reporting of the information, or use of the information, have never been raised by other countries.

Privacy

The collection of such significant volumes of data raises major concerns with regard to security and the privacy of the information in international wire transfers. Security of premises and personnel is paramount at AUSTRAC. Information held by AUSTRAC is securely protected, and disseminated, only in accordance with the law. Access to the database is tightly controlled, and access only allowed for specific purposes both for AUSTRAC personnel, and the personnel of agencies that can have access to the data.

The dissemination of information by AUSTRAC is carefully controlled to ensure that breaches of privacy do not occur. The official information AUSTRAC holds is protected according to the requirements of the *Privacy Act 1988* and *Commonwealth Protective Security Manual*. AUSTRAC continues to maintain the integrity of its information by conducting regular audits and inspections of all classified information to ensure that current standards are maintained, and to ensure that there is not any improper use or disclosure of information.

There are also a number of safeguards and measures in place under legislation to protect official information held by AUSTRAC employees.[11] The legislation provides for penalties if an AUSTRAC employee improperly disseminates information obtained during the course of their duties.

The FTR Act and AML/CTF Act both provide for certain designated people from partner agencies to have access to financial transaction reports for the purposes of performing that agency's functions and powers *only*.[12] Sanctions apply if such a person discloses such AUSTRAC information for an improper purpose. AUSTRAC also maintains logs of all access to its data by AUSTRAC staff and by partner agencies with online staff. Education programs and guidelines have also been issued by AUSTRAC regarding how FTR information may be used, and for privacy and security awareness.

---

[10] See Report at page 61.

[11] See section 25 of the FTR Act and Part 11, Division 4 of the AML/CTF Act.

[12] See section 25 FTR Act, section 70 *Crimes Act 1914*, section 10 *Public Service Act 1999* and section 2.1 of the *Public Service Regulations.*

AUSTRAC has also formally recognised the sharing of FTR via memorandums of understanding ("MOU"). While not legally binding documents, these MOUs are rested within a good faith relationship. MOUs provide the framework within which the AUSTRAC CEO grants access to FTR information and financial intelligence information. In addition, to ensure correct usage of the data, the MOUs contain provision for feedback information advising AUSTRAC of the number of investigations value added, and the value of tax assessments assisted by AUSTRAC financial transaction reports. AUSTRAC has entered into MOUs with 34 partner agencies, and 49 overseas FIUs.

Summary

The mandatory reporting of all customer-based international wire transfers into and out of Australia, has provided AUSTRAC and its partner agencies with an invaluable source of financial intelligence. Tangible evidence is supplied in the number of investigations undertaken by AUSTRAC's law enforcement, national security, revenue and social justice partners, and the amount of taxation revenue resulting directly from use of the information. Proactively identifying criminals in Australia and overseas, through their financial transactions including information as to dates of transactions, locations of transactions, addresses, associates in Australia and overseas, and having this information in real time, has been vital in the investigation and prosecution of the most notorious criminals, both known, and previously unknown, in Australia and in many overseas countries. Issues such as privacy and costs have been resolved inexpensively and to the satisfaction of all parties.

Yours sincerely

Neil J Jensen PSM
Chief Executive Officer

Appendix A

Cases – International Wire Transfers and AUSTRAC

Case 1 – Terrorism financing

This case culminated in the arrest of three members of a terrorist organisation. The trio collectively raised nearly AUD 2 million from an ethnic community in Australia through two organisations - largely through contributions made after the 2004 tsunami in South East Asia. The activities were identified by AUSTRAC's TargIT monitoring system displaying information on **international wire transfers** to South East Asia, South Asia and Western Europe

Case 2 – Importation of drug paraphernalia

A large number of bank drafts valued at between AUD 8,000 and $9,000 were purchased in the names of a number of different entities on behalf of an Australian drug dealer based in Europe. Bank drafts to the sum of more than AUD 2 million were purchased over a short period of time. The bank drafts were to be used for a large import of products relating to the manufacture of drugs in Australia. The drafts purchased in Australia were presented at various banks in Europe, and deposited into bank accounts associated with the drug dealer. Information in the AUSTRAC database also identified related activity and the use of **international wire transfers**. Police forces in a number of countries were involved in the investigation and the drug dealer was imprisoned for 20 years in Europe.

Case 3 - Nigerian 419 Scams

A "Nigerian 419" scam also referred to as an "advance fee fraud" involved scammers contacting an individual by email or letter and, inter alia, offering a share in a large sum of money that they want to transfer out of their country. Scammers seek funds or bank account details to help them transfer the money. AUSTRAC has referred 10 financial intelligence assessment reports involving **international wire transfer** information to an Australian law enforcement agency relating to Nigerian 419 scams. This information has been invaluable for the law enforcement agency in providing them with a greater understanding of the scams themselves, and of the problem in Australia. Significantly, the law enforcement agency is now receiving requests for information from counterparts overseas as a result of AUSTRAC's work.

Case 4 – Investment fraud

Persons purporting to work for overseas firms overseas convinced investors of their authenticity using a number of techniques including the use of appropriate industry jargon, and legitimate businesses. Investors were directed to transfer funds into approximately 20 banks overseas using **international wire transfers**. No investors received a return. Investors became suspicious when fictitious websites were no longer accessible or shut down. Hundreds of Australians invested more than AUD 25 million in the scams. AUSTRAC's **international wire transfer** information was used to identify the movement of funds out of Australia into overseas bank accounts, and identified victims by monitoring **international wire transfer** activity linked to the identified beneficiary accounts overseas as it was occurring, thus enabling potential victims to be warned about the scam. AUSTRAC was also used as a conduit for international FIU requests to South East Asia seeking further information about bank account details and statements.

Case 5 - Drug Smuggling Syndicate Dismantled

An international drug smuggling syndicate spanning Australia, North America and Western Europe was identified by AUSTRAC financial intelligence on outgoing **international wire transfers**. Financial movements surrounding a known drug courier prompted further investigation into the activities of the person which identified a post office box number connected with suspected bank accounts in false names. The false name bank accounts were used in financing ongoing drug couriers entering Australia, by the syndicate.

Case 6 - Cocaine Seized in Oil Filters

This was a joint agency operation leading to the arrest of two people attempting to import two kilograms of cocaine into Australia. AUSTRAC **international wire transfers** were monitored during the course of the investigation and disseminated to the agencies.

Case 7 – Fraud

More than 20 international incoming and outgoing **international wire transfers** totalling more than AUD 80,000 were identified in AUSTRAC's database going to or coming from North America and the central Pacific to an Australian resident. The value of many of the international wire transfers range from under USD 1,000 to USD 4,000. The international wire transfers are linked to a person under investigation in North America for fraud.

Case 8 – Preparing for terrorist acts

A person was convicted for three terrorism offences and was sentenced to 20 years imprisonment. AUSTRAC's database identified **international wire transfers** directed to family members which assisted with identifying different addresses and locations that the prime suspect and others were using.

Case 9 – Revenue and social security fraud

An Australian resident was in receipt of Australian social benefits. AUSTRAC data linked the person to substantial gambling activities. Information in the data also linked the person to a particular company. Multiple addresses for the person became apparent from the transactional information and additional entities were identified. In more than 100 transaction reports to AUSTRAC, more than AUD 20,000 was identified in AUSTRAC **international wire transfers** with a common overseas beneficiary in South East Asia; more than AUD 300,000 was reported in significant cash transaction reports; and, more than AUD 2 million in reports from the gambling venues. The person is being investigated for social security fraud and tax evasion.

Case 10 – Drug trafficking

International wire transfers provided information concerning financial transactions with Europe, Central and North America, and related to suspected cocaine trafficking. The transactions linked with other financial transactions in AUSTRAC's database, provided the names of a range of persons and addresses which enhanced the investigation. A number of persons were charged with attempting to import a commercial quantity of a controlled drug which had a street value of more than AUD 6 million.

Case 11 - Unlicensed financial services business

Over a period of approximately 4 years a person sent more than 10 international wire transfers to different beneficiaries in Oceania totalling AUD 90,000. In the following year the person received 13 incoming **international wire transfers** from Europe totalling nearly AUD 200,000. Two significant cash transactions totalling more than AUD 10,000 were also reported to AUSTRAC in that year. A suspicious activity report was also provided when the person failed to provide evidence of identification when trying to purchase an outgoing international wire transfer. It is alleged that the person, and others, were involved in the operation of an unlicensed financial services business. Approximately 30 affected people, mainly from an ethnic community in Australia, had handed over more than AUD 2 million to the persons.

Case Study 12 – Money laundering

In a case involving the alleged laundering of illicit funds from drug related activity, there was little information available on AUSTRAC's database as the persons used very small value instruments below the cash reporting threshold. One **international wire transfer** however, indicated a small amount of funds being transferred to a trust company in Africa.

Case Study 13 - Restaurant owner's tax bill

An investigation found that a restaurant was paying wages in cash and not remitting "Pay As You Go" tax. Auditors conducted AUSTRAC searches revealing that one of the owners of the restaurant was purchasing multiple international bank drafts with cash, in amounts just below the AUD 10,000 reportable threshold. The drafts were purchased in the names of family, friends and staff members and signed with different signatures and were being sent to relatives overseas. It was found that the owners had been systematically skimming profits from the restaurant and manipulating the cash registers to give incorrect sales readouts. The skimmed funds were then sent to relatives overseas. The money was returned to Australia by **international wire transfers** as 'loans' and interest on these 'loans' was claimed as tax deductions. Amended assessments were issued on all the business owners resulting in approximately AUD 8.4 million in tax and penalties.

Case Study 14 - Customs cracks multi-million dollar duty free fraud

A lengthy investigation into an Australian-based duty free store has been finalised, with the company and its two directors convicted of multi-million dollar fraud charges. It was found that the company had been selling under-bond cigarettes in large quantities for over two years. The extent of these sales enabled the directors to evade taxes of over AUD 2.5 million. AUSTRAC reporting requirements captured a range of financial transaction reports, including **international wire transfers**, involving the entities of interest in this investigation. These reports were submitted by several reporting entities including banks, casinos and exchange bureaus. AUSTRAC's analysis of the data established a network of individuals previously unknown to be linked. A subsequent investigation into the persons of interest uncovered a wider network that also included links to other companies that may have been used to facilitate the fraud. The business and its directors have since been convicted and ordered to repay the AUD 2.5 million in tax that was evaded in addition to penalties in excess of AUD 600,000 and the Commonwealth Government's legal costs of AUD 140,000.

Case 15 - Drug trafficking syndicate dismantled

As part of an ongoing investigation into an alleged money laundering syndicate, Australian Customs Service officers selected a man for examination at Adelaide Airport upon his arrival from Canada in November 2005. The man was searched and allegedly found to be carrying approximately 1.5 kilograms of cocaine. Following his arrest, law enforcement conducted searches at two properties. Subsequent searches led to the seizure of a significant amount of cash and two further arrests. The syndicate was monitored by law enforcement with an alert being placed on the AUSTRAC database to monitor the syndicate's financial activities. Financial transaction reports' (FTR) information, including **international wire transfers**, compiled by AUSTRAC was used to identify the activity and to assist law enforcement in investigation of possible *Proceeds of Crime Act 2002* offences. The three men faced charges including importing a prohibited import and attempting to possess a prohibited import. All men were also charged with dealing with proceeds of crime relating to money or property. The syndicate member carrying the cocaine into Australia pleaded guilty to the offences of importing a prohibited import and was sentenced to six years with a non-parole period of four years. Another member of the syndicate received a six-month suspended sentence with a two-year good behaviour bond for possession of cash which was reasonably expected to be the proceeds of crime.

Case 16 - Mail interception leads to trafficking and laundering charges

A dubious international mail package from Canada was intercepted as a result of intelligence developed by the Australian Customs Service. On further inspection the package contained an illegal precursor drug used to manufacture amphetamines. This intelligence linked the homeowner, who had previously been convicted of a similar offence, to the illegal importation. A search was conducted of the person of interest's residence with several assets including cash, a diamond ring and a motor vehicle confiscated, in addition to further funds located in a safety deposit box. Analysis of AUSTRAC information revealed that the suspect had opened several accounts under their own name and also in false names. Financial transaction reports' information also showed suspicious activity reports (SARs) profiling structuring activity where the suspect was deliberately depositing cash under AUD 10,000 in order to avoid the reporting obligation. The SARs not only identified structuring activity, they also highlighted the alleged use of third parties to undertake structuring of deposits and **international wire transfers** on behalf of the suspect. Following the investigation the suspect pleaded guilty to one count of importing prohibited imports under section 400.3 (1) of the *Criminal Code Act 1995*, and was sentenced to six years and two months with a non-parole period of four years. The suspect also pleaded guilty to a number of money laundering offences and the use of bank accounts in false names. The cash and other items of property seized amounted to a total in excess of AUD 350,000 forfeited to the Commonwealth Government.

Case 17 - AUSTRAC information led to arrests of multi-million dollar money launderers

A multi-million dollar money laundering syndicate was dismantled following the dissemination of information held by AUSTRAC to a joint task force. The investigation into the activities of a currency exchange business culminated in the arrest of four people who were charged with numerous money laundering and structuring offences. At the initial phase of the investigation, the suspicious activities of the currency exchange business and associated persons were detected through financial transaction reports' information, including **international wire transfers**. Financial investigators interrogated the AUSTRAC database throughout the course of the investigation with significant results. Searches of account numbers were able to assist in establishing relevant details of transactions and identifying associates. A number of suspicious activity reports relevant to the investigation highlighted transactions that were alleged to have been deliberately structured to fall below the cash transaction reporting limit in an attempt to avoid reporting obligations. A number of search warrants were executed simultaneously on the premises of the currency exchange business and the persons associated. A total of AUD 47, 500 was seized during the execution of the search warrants and approximately AUD 247,000 in assets are the subject of a Commonwealth Government injunction.

Case 18 - $8 million cold calling case

Authorities received numerous complaints regarding a "cold calling" fraud which had been targeting Australians. Victims had been approached to invest a total of AUD 8 million in 'heating oil options', 'gasoline options' and 'gold bullion options' purportedly traded on non-existent foreign currency exchanges. The unsuspecting investors had been instructed to remit funds into a number of company accounts located in Malaysia and Hong Kong. AUSTRAC **international wire transfer** reports identified that a portion of the transmitted funds were being returned to Australian-based beneficiary accounts. The account holders were identified as being a Malaysian businessman, and an Australian student who both held accounts with major banking institutions. The student allegedly used the received funds to purchase AUD 100,000 worth of bonds. AUSTRAC information demonstrated that the activity had only been occurring for a short time before investigations began, suggesting it had only been in operation for a short period of time. As the accounts and bonds fall under Australian jurisdiction they have effectively been frozen, awaiting further investigation into the scheme.

Case 19 - Former Directors of unregistered company imprisoned

An Australian law enforcement agency investigation commenced after information was received through various sources regarding an unregistered managed investment scheme. AUSTRAC financial transaction reports' information was valuable in the initial stages of the investigation in that it identified the targeted entities. A trust and its trustee company as well as various other entities and their addresses were identified in South Australia. It was apparent from AUSTRAC **international wire transfer** data that the targeted entities had been transferring significant funds to New Zealand. As a result of the positive results found on the relevant entities, an AUSTRAC alert was placed on the trust and other entities for the duration of the investigation. The AUSTRAC alert was used to identify any additional funds being raised by previously unidentified entities and sent offshore to the unregistered managed investment scheme. As the investigation continued, investigators found that the trust had received money from 94 investors in Australia and New Zealand and placed the money into unregistered projects in New Zealand and the United States of America. Financial transaction reports' data assisted in identifying that approximately AUD 5.8 million of the funds had been lost in these unregistered operations. The investors were mainly retirees and operators of self-managed superannuation funds. Two people each pleaded guilty to a charge of operating an unregistered managed investment scheme under the *Corporations Act 2001*. Person A was sentenced in October 2003 to 20 months imprisonment with a non-parole period of six months, and then to be released under the supervision of a Corrections Officer for 12 months. Person B was sentenced to 14 months imprisonment, to be released immediately upon entering into a bond and being supervised in the same terms as Person A.

Case Study 20 - FTR information assists the US Internal Revenue Service

One of the monitoring tools used by AUSTRAC is "Aggcells". **The international wire transfers** are the subject of reports generated by this tool and highlight monthly variations in the flow of funds between Australia and other countries. The Aggcells monthly report is provided to an Australian Taxation Office (ATO) analyst who examines it with a view to identifying unusual transactions or trends. These unusual transactions or trends normally involve tax haven countries. An ATO analyst noted a sizeable increase in funds being wired to Australia from a small tax haven country during a particular month. Further investigation identified that a particular individual had been receiving a large amount of these funds and had received around AUD 18 million over the past five years. Checks on various databases showed that the person had not lodged tax returns for a number of years and the case was referred to an auditor in the ATO's "Serious Non Compliance Service Business Line" compliance department. The task of this audit was to ascertain if the person was an Australian resident, and also to establish if the AUD 18 million, which had been remitted to his Australian bank account, was assessable income for Australian taxation purposes. Interviews with the person established that he was a professional gambler who had developed a program to select winning horses for a business that operated from an offshore tax haven. Immigration checks on his international movements confirmed that the person was not an Australian resident for income tax purposes. Following discussions with various other branches of the ATO, it was decided that information obtained during the course of the audit should be provided to the Internal Revenue Service (IRS) in the United States of America. Information from the ATO's enquiries was then disseminated under the Exchange of Information provisions of the Australia/United States of America Double Tax agreement. On receipt of the information the IRS conducted their own enquiries, raising assessments against the individual and collecting more than USD 5 million in unpaid taxes.

Case Study 21 - Laundering of drug proceeds through debit card facilities

Following the dissemination of financial transaction reports (FTR) information by AUSTRAC to a law enforcement agency, an AUSTRAC alert was raised on a suspect and his associate. The FTR information related to a student who on a number of occasions loaded structured amounts of $9,900, to avoid the reporting requirements of the *Financial Transactions Reports* Act *1988*, onto debit cards in his own name and that of his associate. The suspect had previously come to the notice of law enforcement agencies in relation to a cocaine seizure at Sydney Airport in 2001 which he was alleged to have organised. Following further research and intelligence gathering, a joint operation commenced, involving two law enforcement agencies. A further 15 FTRs were recorded on the AUSTRAC database, showing both the suspect and his associate conducting deposits of structured amounts onto debit cards. Within two months they loaded a total of over AUD 100, 000 onto two debit cards. AUSTRAC's automated monitoring system also detected a further series of **international wire transfers** linked to both targets. An assessment of FTR information was disseminated to the law enforcement agencies and assisted the investigation, resulting in the arrest of both targets. In late 2003 the associate departed Brisbane for South America and returned to Brisbane from another South American destination 12 days later with approximately 5.8 kilograms of cocaine in his baggage. He later admitted that he had previously brought drugs into Australia on two occasions for a payment of AUD 8, 000 each time. He was arrested and charged with importing and possessing a prohibited import. The suspect was also charged a couple of months later with alleged conspiracy to bring into Australia approximately 5.8 kilograms of cocaine with an additional charge of structuring cash transactions and laundering almost AUD 400,000. He was found guilty and sentenced to seven years imprisonment

Case Study 22 - 300 kilograms of cocaine seized

AUSTRAC **international wire transfer** information was pivotal in initiating various operations which related to the importation of cocaine into Australia from South America. This investigation started in 1998 when financial transaction reports' (FTR) information was reported on Mr Y, the alleged importer of cocaine. Subsequent research indicated that six structured international wire transfers had occurred between February and April 1998. Further in-depth financial analysis using the AUSTRAC database showed significant international wire transfers to the Middle East and to various countries in Europe, believed to be payment for the cocaine. Mr X was identified as the overseas beneficiary of these international wire transfers. This particular investigation concluded in December 1998 without any charges being laid, but the intelligence collected was further developed by Australian law enforcement agencies. Investigators later analysed the FTR information identified in the earlier investigation which led to further operational work. This resulted in the seizure of a package containing cocaine and led to the conviction of three people. A number of international wires transfers, believed to be payment for the cocaine were produced as evidence in this trial. As a result of inquiries by law enforcement agencies the entities of interest in the previous two operations had again come to notice for the importation of sandstone blocks from South America. A joint operation consisting of three agencies commenced in April 2000 which led to the identification of Mr X for whom an outstanding arrest warrant on drug related charges existed. A search of his premises located almost AUD 300, 000 cash in plastic shopping bags. Further searches of the garage adjoining the premises located four plastic drums containing round blocks of white powder wrapped in plastic. Police seized in total over 300 kilograms of cocaine, making it the largest ever drug seizure in the state. In March 2004 Mr X, an overseas based businessman, was found guilty of importing the drugs and following an unsuccessful appeal received a sentence of 20 years imprisonment with a non-parole period of 14 years.

Case 23 Laundering the proceeds of internet banking theft

Law enforcement arrested a person in Perth Australia who was involved in laundering the proceeds of internet banking theft. A person stole funds over a period of 12 months and used multiple bank accounts to launder AUD 60,000. In one instance, the person received AUD 10,000, which was withdrawn from their bank account and sent to criminals in Eastern Europe using **international wire transfers**. The person also opened a number of bank accounts with different banking institutions and sent the account numbers to contacts in Eastern Europe, allowing them to directly withdraw money via the internet from the Australian accounts.

Case 24 Drug network undertakes multiple structured wire transfers

A person facilitated the structuring of over 1,500 cash deposits and **international wire transfers** utilising a network of associates. The associates would travel from one bank branch to the next on the same day, making deposits using false names and addresses. The wire transfers were deposited into numerous overseas bank accounts controlled by local criminals in that jurisdiction. Each deposit would be under the AUD 10,000 reporting limit in order to avoid AUSTRAC and law enforcement detection. The estimated total amount of funds transferred was in excess of AUD 14 million. On occasion, in excess of AUD100,000 was sent overseas in one day.

Case 25 Company directors generate false receipts to evade tax

Directors of a company were involved in purchasing large quantities of duty free cigarettes and alcohol to sell on the domestic market contrary to their export-duty free status, thus avoiding tax obligations. By not paying any tax on the goods the company was able to markedly increase profits. The syndicate also generated false receipts that purported to come from an export company detailing their alleged cigarette exports. Investigations into the company confirmed that no such exports had ever been made. Payment for the cigarettes was made to the delivery driver on a cash-on-delivery basis. A large number of the company's sales occurred over the internet from customers paying via credit card. Payments for these orders were made from one of two credit cards linked to Belize bank accounts. One of these cards was held in the company's name. The money in the Belize bank account was sent there by one of the directors using several false names from Australia, Vietnam, Belize, and Hong Kong. The director conducted structured **international wire transfers** under false names and from company accounts. The funds were deposited at well known banks, with multiple transactions occurring on the same day at different bank locations, and all of the cash transfers were conducted in amounts of just under AUD10,000 to avoid the reporting threshold.

Case 26 Broker used to facilitate money laundering

An account was opened in a particular country in a false name. **International wire transfers** from third parties located in tax haven countries were transferred into the account, almost always under the AUD10, 000 reporting threshold. The customer faxed instructions to the broker to transfer money to third party accounts in the United States, including three different accounts at three different banks on the same day.

Case 27 Fraud money invested in securities market

A brokerage firm opened several accounts for a group of 12 linked individuals, including a non-resident account that was used to record very large movements and apparently to centralise most of the suspected flows, which totalled more than USD18 million. The launderers used the following two mechanisms:

- the accounts of some of the parties involved were credited with large sums received from countries of concern, which were invested in the stocks of listed companies in a particular country;

- the accounts of the individuals concerned were credited with sums from regions of concern, which were transferred to the non-resident account (the first accounts were used as screens).

This securities buy/sell mechanism was used to filter the flows through the broker and then the clearer and custodian. Once filtered, the funds were sent to locations via **international wire transfers** in regions of concern and offshore financial centres. This information showed that the co-opted broker had been used to launder the proceeds from various forms of frauds. The manager of the brokerage firm served as a relay for the criminal organisations involved.

Case 28 Cash couriers used to launder funds

AUSTRAC information identified a series of financial transactions where a person appeared to have been conducting them in such a way as to avoid the reporting threshold of the *Financial Transaction Reports Act 1988*. Financial transaction reports' (FTRs) showed that more than AUD 4 million was remitted by one person to accounts at two different banks in Asia. After it received AUSTRAC's information, an Australian law enforcement agency commenced an investigation into the possible money laundering activities of the subject of these reports. The person was already known to law enforcement agencies. After several months of investigation, information was received specifying that the person was collecting money from an associate then remitting the funds to Asia via a particular cash dealer. The person was observed attending an associate's premises before driving towards the cash dealer's business premises. The person was intercepted and found to be in possession of approximately AUD 50,000 cash. The person was subsequently arrested and during an interview, investigators learned that a resident in Asia paid the person a commission in return for the remittance of funds to Asia. It was further ascertained that packages of AUD 100, 000 cash were delivered within Australia and subsequently electronically remitted overseas through a series of structured transactions involving **international wire transfers**. In court, the person pleaded guilty to one count of money laundering and one count of defrauding the Commonwealth Government and was found guilty on a second count of defrauding the Commonwealth. He was sentenced to a maximum of six months imprisonment for money laundering and 12 months imprisonment for defrauding the Commonwealth Government. As a result of this investigation, a tax assessment of approximately AUD 4 million was raised and more than AUD 600, 000 has been recovered.

Case 29 Businessman defrauds Commonwealth Government and sends funds offshore

A revenue agency initiated an operation after receiving a suspicious activity report (SAR) referred to them by AUSTRAC. Suspicions were raised as the subject of the SAR, a small businessman, was found to be in receipt of a large amount of government funds. AUSTRAC information was used to identify transactions conducted by the businessman, highlighting the fact that he was sending funds offshore via **international wire transfers** to Africa. A further four SARs were received by AUSTRAC, showing that the person was structuring his withdrawals in an attempt to avoid detection by AUSTRAC. These reports also indicated the person's intention to leave the country permanently for an overseas destination. Under section 16(4) of the *Financial Transactions Reports Act 1988*, the revenue agency served a notice on the cash dealer involved to gather more information regarding the person. As a result of further enquiries, it was found that the person had defrauded the Commonwealth Government of over AUD 100,000. The revenue agency sought the assistance of an Australian law enforcement agency to arrest the person two days before he was due to leave Australia. The person was charged with two counts of obtaining a financial benefit by deception under section 134.2(1) of the *Criminal Code 1995*. Subsequently, he was found guilty and was sentenced to one year's imprisonment on the first offence and two-and-a-half year's imprisonment on the second offence, with a minimum term of 10 months to be served. Without the cash dealer's report, their suspicions and consequently AUSTRAC's referral of the SAR, which highlighted the occurrence of an offence, the person would have remained undetected and would have left Australia.

Case 30 'Night clubbers' used to send funds offshore

Persons of interest were involved in a cocaine importation secreted in clothing consignments from New York using a parcel courier service. Prior to each importation, **international wire transfers** were sent to accounts in the United States (US). These transfers were conducted by individuals who were recruited by the persons of interest at night clubs to send money on their behalf. The funds were sent to individuals and company accounts held in the US in amounts ranging from AUD 6, 000-19,995. The currency of the transactions also alternated between USD and AUD.

Case 31 Wire transfers used as primary source of funding drugs

AUSTRAC information initiated a joint investigation that led to the seizure of narcotics imported from Europe. Financial transaction reports' (FTR) information related to this investigation helped to identify the overseas based beneficiary of the **international wire** transfers as the main source of the narcotics. Other Australian associates were also identified from FTR information as they were sending funds to the same beneficiary. Key information in the form of domestic and overseas addresses and accounts was also discovered from the FTRs.

The FTRs were significant in determining the involvement of the persons in the financing of the imported narcotics. In addition to this, a suspicious activity report lodged on one of the suspects confirmed links to persons associated with the narcotics seizure. As a result three persons were found guilty, and one person pleaded guilty to being knowingly concerned with the importation of a prohibited import contrary to section 233B (1) (d) of the *Customs Act 1901*. The jail terms ranged from four months to nine years.

Case 32 Wire transfers and e-gold payments used to purchase stolen bank details

Persons of interest were involved in the purchase of stolen bank account and credit card details from Russia and Eastern Europe via the internet. These were purchased through **international wire transfers** of approximately AUD2,000 and by way of e-gold payments. The principal person of interest was arrested on 26 fraud and computer crime offences in relation to using these bank details to withdraw funds without authorisation in internet transfers to accounts of associates. AUSTRAC searches revealed that a person in this syndicate had a history of alleged involvement in internet bank fraud through phishing. A laptop seized at the arrest of the principal person revealed details of **international wire transfers** transacted through remittance dealers and e-gold. Russian and other recipients identified from these transactions facilitated the identification of additional persons from AUSTRAC information.

Case 33 Criminal funds laundered through payment of insurance premiums

A company director set up a money laundering scheme involving two companies, each one established under two different legal systems involving **international wire transfers**. Both of the entities were to provide financial services and providing financial guarantees for which he would act as director. These companies wired the sum of USD 1.1 million to the accounts of the company director in Country S. It is likely that the funds originated from some sort of criminal activity. Funds were transferred from one account to another (several types of accounts were involved, including both current and savings accounts). Through one of these **international wire transfers,** the funds were transferred to Country U from a current account in order to make payments on life insurance policies. The investment in these policies was the main mechanism in the scheme for laundering the funds. The premiums paid for the life insurance policies in Country U amounted to some USD 1.2 million and represented the last step in the laundering operation.

Case 34 Understated income siphoned to overseas bank accounts

In an organised tax evasion scam, two brothel owners withheld cash takings, understated their income and siphoned funds via **international wire transfers** to overseas bank accounts over a three-year period. The offenders obtained false identification documents and structured the transfers using false identities and names of associates. One of the offenders then changed his method of laundering the cash payments, possibly as a result of his growing awareness of the role and function of AUSTRAC. Methods included the physical carriage of cash out of Australia, the purchase of bullion, acquisition of prestigious motor vehicles, and loans to associates.

Case 35 Smuggling of gold to evade tax

Paul was a well-known customer of a European bank. On a number of occasions he purchased gold bullion from the bank in ingots of one kilogram with the explanation that he was buying the gold to export directly to a foreign company. Paul transported the gold out of the bank by himself after each transaction. In a single year he purchased a total of more than 800 kilograms of gold with a value of more than USD 7 million. The gold was paid for by funds drawn from his company account. The bank was also able to see that at regular intervals funds were transferred into the account from another company in a neighbouring country, as one would expect. However, Paul's actions in transporting the gold himself seemed unusual to the bank, and the bank officials decided to disclose their concerns to the national FIU. The FIU researched Paul and his company within various law enforcement intelligence databases, but no obvious link to criminality could be found. However, the scale of the gold purchases justified a formal investigation by the FIU, and further enquiries were undertaken. These enquiries revealed that Paul was not in fact selling the gold to a foreign company as claimed. Before buying the gold, Paul always met with a foreign citizen named Daniel. Although they drove to the bank together in Paul's car, Daniel never entered the bank. After Paul purchased the gold, they drove to Daniel's car and hid the gold in the boot. Then Daniel drove back to his own country, crossing the border without declaring the bullion at Customs and therefore avoiding paying import duties. Once in his own country, Daniel handed the gold over to Andrew, who delivered it to another company for sale on the open market. A proportion of the profits from the sale of the gold were transferred back to Daniel's company via **international wire transfers**, from which he drew the next tranche of funds to purchase more gold. The amount of additional profit generated by this simple tax evasion scheme was substantial. At the time of writing, criminal proceedings for money laundering in conjunction with tax evasion were being raised against Paul, Daniel and Andrew. The smuggling operation was estimated to have caused tax losses to the government of some USD 1 million. Because the proceeds from selling the smuggled gold were obtained illegally, the judicial authorities in the FIU's country have also begun criminal proceedings against the individuals involved.

Case 36 Criminal attempts to launder fraud proceeds through the diamond market

A known criminal who had benefited financially from a fraud that took place in another country attempted to send money via **international wire transfers** to jewellers to purchase precious stones. The financial institution holding the account had been concerned about the individual for some time and had made several suspicious activity reports to the FIU. The client attempted to send USD 8.2 million to the jewellers. Before this took place the bank took the commercial decision to freeze the accounts. The law enforcement agency made initial investigations and was satisfied that the attempt to buy precious stones had been an attempt to launder the proceeds of the fraud.

Case 37 Financial controller launders funds through bookmaker

A person in control of a corporation's financial affairs abused this position of trust by defrauding the company. The person authorised and instructed staff to make electronic funds transfers from the company to his bookmakers' accounts. He then instructed the bookmakers to direct excess funds and winnings from their accounts to his account or third party accounts, and instructed bank officers to transfer funds from his accounts via **international wire transfers**. In order to layer and disguise the fraud, he instructed his lawyer to contact the beneficiary of the original international transfers to return the payments via wire transfers into the lawyer's trust account. Approximately AUD 450, 000 was returned in one **international wire transfer** to the lawyer's trust account. The lawyer then transferred AUD350, 000 to a church fund in an attempt to further hide the assets and was preparing to transfer the funds to an overseas account. To access these funds the person made structured withdrawals of AUD 9,000 each within a nine day period.

Case 38 Solicitor coordinates u-turn transactions to legitimise funds

An Australian-based solicitor structured funds to an offshore account in Hong Kong. At times it is believed that he actually carried cash to Hong Kong. His colleague, a Hong Kong-based solicitor, arranged for the creation of offshore companies in the British Virgin Islands and bank accounts in Hong Kong to receive structured funds from Australia. These funds were then transferred to other countries by the Hong Kong-based solicitor by **international wire transfers** to hide from authorities or returned to Australia in order to appear legitimate.

Case 39 Gatekeepers used in web of criminal activity

This case involved the production of large quantities of amphetamines in several states of Australia. The suspects laundered most of the proceeds of the manufacture of the amphetamine with the assistance of Australian entities. The Australian-based entities deposited cash supplied to them by the wife of the main suspect (usually in structured amounts under the AUD 10, 000 reporting threshold) into their own accounts. The funds were drawn from the accounts using cheques payable to the suspect's wife or a company or business over which she and her husband had control.

The Australian-based entities were also instructed to send some of the money to overseas accounts by **international wire transfer.** Money was often moved through different accounts, before being wire transferred offshore. The case involved approximately AUD 5 million. Over AUD 1 million was also laundered by the group through an accountancy firm. The firm was initially approached on the basis that one of the suspects had substantial funds overseas, which he wished to repatriate to Australia. At the time, the person was a bankrupt and money could not be held in his own name.

Advice was sought from the accountants to devise a structure to enable the repatriation of the funds and acquisition of real estate. The accountants were given AUD 20, 000 to be used as a deposit on a real estate purchase. The accountants were aware of reporting thresholds and deposited the money into bank accounts in amounts less than the AUD 10, 000 reporting threshold. The accountants recommended a number of money laundering schemes to the principals of the drug ring. Their standard approach was to launder the money into a number of bank accounts in amounts less than the reporting threshold of AUD 10, 000 and to then draw cheques on those accounts. The accountants used 15 different bank accounts to receive the cash. These included personal accounts, the bank accounts of others, unwitting family members, the accountants' business accounts (including trust accounts), and the bank accounts of corporate entities established for the purpose.

Two other methods used to launder the funds were use of bookmakers and gamblers. In the case of the bookmakers, the method was to attend race days with substantial amounts of cash. The person would seek out a bookmaker he knew, express his discomfort at carrying such a large amount in cash and ask them to hold his cash for him until he either used it for bets or collected it at the end of the day. He would then leave it with the bookmaker and deliberately not collect it at the end of the day. Early the following week he would contact the bookmaker and ask him to post him a cheque for the money. The accountants had a business association with a wealthy businessman who was a frequent gambler at Australian casinos. The accountants approached the businessman and offered to provide cash at short notice to him or his associates for gambling at casinos. The accountants offered to accept 95 per cent of the value of the cash they provided on the basis that the gambler later repaid the money by depositing money into a foreign bank account which had been set up for the purpose.

Appendix B: Examples of US Wire Fraud cases involving overseas jurisdictions

1. Brett Wolf "Pigeon-aided bank fraud case underscores importance of AML software", 5 February 2008, *Complinet;*

http://www.complinet.com/global/news/news/article.html?ref=101796&high=international+ wire+transfer+cases

2. "Two money laundering suspects face rearrest", 27 November 2007, Global Press Service;

http://www.complinet.com/global/news/news/article.html?ref=99684&high=international+wi re+transfer+cases

3. Brett Wolf, "Laundering scam finally appears on FBI's radar", 24 August 2007, *Complinet;*

http://www.complinet.com/global/news/news/article.html?ref=96180&high=international+wi re+transfer+cases

4. Chris Hamblin, "Former Comverse chief escapes to Israel with disputed money", 22 August 2006, *Complinet;*

http://www.complinet.com/global/news/news/article.html?ref=82637&high=international+wi re+transfer+cases

5. Brett Wolf, "Florida stamps out food stamp fraud", 25 January 2006, *Complinet*

http://www.complinet.com/global/news/news/article.html?ref=76872&high=international+wi re+transfer+cases

6. Brett Wolf, "Money laundering compliance officer indicted for money laundering", 25 April 2005, *Complinet*

http://www.complinet.com/global/news/news/article.html?ref=70080&high=international+wi re+transfer+cases

7. Brett Wolf "San Francisco men accused of wiring fraud proceeds to Russia" 7 February 2008, *Complinet;*
http://www.complinet.com/global/news/news/article.html?ref=101891&highlight=WIRE+F RAUD&ephigh=

8. Brett Wolf, "US and Dutch authorities bring down advance-fee fraudsters" 1 February 2008, *Complinet;*

http://www.complinet.com/global/news/news/article.html?ref=101660&highlight=WIRE+F RAUD&ephigh=

9. "Florida man sues bank over $90K wire fraud", 8 February 2005, *The Register*

www.the register.co.uk/2005/02/08/e-banking_trojanlawsuit/-29k

10. US v David Bermingham, Giles Darby, and Gary Mulgrew

news.findlaw.com/hdocs/docs/enron/usbrmnghm91202ind.pdf

11. Benedict P. Kuehne "Two others indicted on money laundering charges", 7 February 2008, *Newswire*

http://global.factiva.com/redir/default.aspx?p=sta&ep=em&an=PRN0000020080207e427008
0207e4270089a&fid=10544837&cat=a2aid=9AUS006900&ns=18&fn=Money%20Launderi
ng&ft=g&qt=g

12. Brett Wolf "Californian lawyer admits masterminding international 'loan-back'
scheme"30 January 2008, *Complinet*;

http://www.complinet.com/global/news/news/article.html?ref=101610&high=WIRE+FRAU
D

13. Helen O'Gorman "Texan investigators unearth suspected $7.8m laundry", 10 January
2008, *Complinet*.

http://www.complinet.com/global/news/news/article.html?ref=100895&high=WIRE+FRAU
D

14. Brett Wolf "New York rabbi and associates indicted for tax fraud and laundering", 20
December 2007, *Complinet*

http://www.complinet.com/global/news/news/article.html?ref=100489&high=WIRE+FRAU
D

15. "Two money laundering suspects face rearrest",27 November 2007, Global Press Service

http://www.complinet.com/global/news/news/article.html?ref=99684&high=WIRE+FRAUD

16. Brett Wolf," US prosecutors charge six in international securities fraud and money
laundering scheme", 22 October 2007, *Complinet*

http://www.complinet.com/global/news/news/article.html?ref=98224&high=WIRE+FRAUD

17. Brett Wolf , "US man gets seven years for international ID theft and laundering scheme",
20 August 2007, *Complinet*

http://www.complinet.com/global/news/news/article.html?ref=96012&high=WIRE+FRAUD

18 Brett Wolf, "US retiree reclaims money from Canadian fraudsters", 21 August 2007,
Complinet

Bhttp://www.complinet.com/global/news/news/article.html?ref=95405&high=WIRE+FRAU
Dett Wolf in Miami

19. Brett Wolf, "Woman jailed for laundering $1.9m stolen from Government of Bermuda",
29 June 2007, *Complinet*

http://www.complinet.com/global/news/news/article.html?ref=94232&high=WIRE+FRAUD

20. Brett Wolf, "Former US county official sentenced to 14 years in prison" 22 June 2007,
Complinet

http://www.complinet.com/global/news/news/article.html?ref=93973&high=WIRE+FRAUD

21. Brett Wolf, "Funds transfer companies indicted for 'fooling' banks over gambling transactions" 16 May 2007, *Complinet*

http://www.complinet.com/global/news/news/article.html?ref=92456&high=WIRE+FRAUD

23. Brett Wolf, "Bank fraudster wired proceeds to South America", 1 May 2007, *Complinet*

http://www.complinet.com/global/news/news/article.html?ref=91795&high=WIRE+FRAUD

23. Brett Wolf, "Forex trading guru indicted for fraud and laundering", 10 April 2007, *Complinet*

http://www.complinet.com/global/news/news/article.html?ref=90784&high=WIRE+FRAUD

24. Brett Wolf, "Fraudsters wired hundreds of thousands of dollars to Jordan say US prosecutors", 30 March 2007, *Complinet;*

http://www.complinet.com/global/news/news/article.html?ref=90492&high=WIRE+FRAUD

25. Brett Wolf, "US-Hungarian task force brings down eBay fraud and laundering operation", 29 March 2007, *Complinet*

26. Brett Wolf, "Alert bank officers help stop county official's alleged corruption", 20 February 2007, *Complinet*

http://www.complinet.com/global/news/news/article.html?ref=89220&high=WIRE+FRAUD

27. Brett Wolf, "Five Americans indicted for theft of Iraq reconstruction funds", 9 February 2007,

http://www.complinet.com/global/news/news/article.html?ref=88959&high=WIRE+FRAUD

28. Brett Wolf, "Bank fraud may have helped fund Al Qaeda in Iraq", 23 October 2006, *Complinet*

http://www.complinet.com/global/news/news/article.html?ref=84438&high=WIRE+FRAUD

29. Brett Wolf, "HSBC insider implicated in $30m scheme", 8 September 2006, *Complinet*

http://www.complinet.com/global/news/news/article.html?ref=83197&high=WIRE+FRAUD

30. Brett Wolf, "California charges mortgage head with fraud and laundering", 5 September 2006, *Complinet*

http://www.complinet.com/global/news/news/article.html?ref=83005&high=WIRE+FRAUD

31. Brett Wolf, "Information issued by US Attorney's Office for Maryland on Dec 14: Indonesian man sentenced for conspiracy to provide material support to foreign terrorist organisation, money laundering, attempted export of arms ", 14 December 2007, US Fed News

http://global.factiva.com/ha/default.aspx

32. Brett Wolf, "Arizona men charged with stock fraud and money laundering", 16 May 2006, *Complinet*

http://www.complinet.com/global/news/news/article.html?ref=79901&high=WIRE+FRAUD

33. Brett Wolf, "Philippine authorities will deport US citizen", 3 May 2006, *Complinet*

http://www.complinet.com/global/news/news/article.html?ref=79564&high=WIRE+FRAUD

34. Chris Raphael," Fraudsters use white-out to take bank for $8.9m" 8 March 2006, *Complinet*

http://www.complinet.com/global/news/news/article.html?ref=78120&high=WIRE+FRAUD

(This page intentionally left blank)

Financial Transactions and
Reports Analysis
Centre of Canada

Centre d'analyse des
opérations et déclarations
financières du Canada

Ottawa, Canada K1P 1H7

Office of the Director   Cabinet du directeur

March 25, 2008

Mr. James H. Freis, Jr.
Director
Financial Crimes Enforcement Network
Post Office Box 39
Vienna, Virginia 22183
United States of America

Dear Mr. Freis:

I understand that the Financial Crimes Enforcement Network (FinCEN) has been
exploring the feasibility of adding a cross-border electronic funds transfer (EFT)
reporting regime to its operations. It is in consideration of this exercise, and in the
spirit of collaboration, that we at the Financial Transactions and Reports Analysis
Centre of Canada (FINTRAC) wish to share the positive experience that we have had
with our own implementation of such a regime in 2002. We hope that this
letter will demonstrate the great benefits that EFT data collection can bring to the
development of financial intelligence.

This letter provides an overview of Canada's EFT reporting regime, as well as a
demonstration of the very positive impact that EFT reports have had on FINTRAC's
financial intelligence.

Canada's EFT Reporting Regime:

Canada's *Proceeds of Crime (Money Laundering) and Terrorist Financing
Regulations* (Regulations) require that financial entities[1] and money services
businesses (MSBs) in Canada report all international EFTs[2] in amounts of $10,000 or
more – entering or leaving Canada - to FINTRAC, no later than five working days
after the day of the transfer. These regulations were enacted in 2002, and the

.../2

---

[1] Financial entities that report EFTs include banks, savings and credit unions, caisses
populaires, cooperative credit societies, and trust and loan companies.
[2] An electronic funds transfer (EFT), as defined in the Regulations, is the transmission of
instructions for a transfer of funds, other than the transfer of funds within Canada, through
any electronic, magnetic or optical device, telephone instrument or computer.

Canadä

implementation of Canada's EFT reporting regime took place over the course of the 2002-2003 fiscal year, beginning with the reporting of SWIFT transactions in June 2002 and following up with the reporting of all other EFTs in March 2003.

FINTRAC worked with those entities that would be affected by these new reporting requirements to develop a reporting scheme that would accommodate both the large processing systems used by major banks, as well as those used by lower volume reporters. It was determined that entities needed the option of an on-line system that permitted them to either file individual reports, one at a time, or allowed them to group reports together and provide FINTRAC with a "batch" of reports of up to 10,000 at a time.

Following consultations with the larger institutions who would be most affected by these new reporting requirements, the government of Canada agreed to create a report form that included many fields contained in a SWIFT[3] message. By accepting many fields from the SWIFT form and requiring institutions to add only minimal additional information in their possession, we have been able to greatly minimize the resources that they have had to dedicate in order to comply with the Regulations, while successfully maximizing their electronic reporting.

Since June 2002, SWIFT members have been required to submit SWIFT EFT Reports to FINTRAC, whenever EFTs of $10,000 or more are transmitted as SWIFT MT 100[4] or MT 103 messages. The regulatory requirements are aligned with the information that is generally included in SWIFT EFT Reports. Essentially, entities who transfer funds via the SWIFT network submit to FINTRAC a copy of the SWIFT message. These reports contain comprehensive information on transactions, such as specific data on all parties involved in the transaction (including information on the sender and receiver of the EFTs, institutions and all third parties involved in the transfer, information on accounts and some additional payment information). Attached to this letter are the relevant schedules from the Regulations that list the specific reporting requirements for outgoing and incoming SWIFT messages. Currently, there are 31 SWIFT members in Canada reporting such reports to FINTRAC, including 29 banks.

It is important to note that not all entities who report EFTs to FINTRAC are SWIFT members. EFTs not routed through the SWIFT network are also required to be reported electronically to FINTRAC as Non-SWIFT reports. The required data fields

.../3

---

[3] SWIFT means the Society for Worldwide Interbank Financial Telecommunication. The SWIFT network is the data processing system that is used most often by the international banking community to send EFTs.

[4] A reportable EFT includes the SWIFT MT 100 message. However, this type of message was removed from the SWIFT network in November 2003.

in these reports are similar to those in the SWIFT EFT reports and entities submitting these reports do so through FINTRAC's on-line reporting tool, either individually or as a "batch". The relevant schedules from the Regulations that list the specific requirements for Non-SWIFT EFT reports to FINTRAC are also attached to this letter.

With these two approaches, reports of international EFTs of $10,000 or more are received by FINTRAC and downloaded daily into its database for analysis. From April 1, 2002 to March 31, 2007, FINTRAC received 36.5 million EFT reports. Of these reports, over 15 million were SWIFT and slightly more than 21 million were non-SWIFT.

In order to meet Canada's privacy requirements, strict security measures have been implemented to ensure the utmost privacy protection for the information that is reported to FINTRAC.

Thanks to careful preparations and cooperative testing exercises with major reporting entities, FINTRAC achieved its goal of a streamlined, highly secure data collection system that is easily used by the entities that are subject to EFT reporting requirements.

Benefits of a Cross-Border EFT Reporting System

The contribution of EFT reports to FINTRAC case development cannot be understated. Since first receiving these reports, FINTRAC has increasingly made use of this data in developing cases and making case disclosures of suspected money laundering and terrorist activity financing. In 2002-2003, 41% of all FINTRAC cases contained EFT reports. By 2005-2006 this percentage had almost doubled to 77%. Indeed, EFT reports have proven to be valuable to FINTRAC's financial intelligence product. In 2006-2007, FINTRAC completed a total of 193 case disclosures, 86% of which contained EFT reports.

The relative contribution that EFT reports add to the various types of cases is quite substantial as well. For example, FINTRAC made 152 money laundering disclosures in 2006-2007, 84% of which included EFT reports. Perhaps most remarkably, 91% of terrorist activity financing and threats to the security of Canada disclosures made by FINTRAC in that fiscal year included EFT reports. Many of these wires were sent to locations of specific concern, whether with respect to a specific terrorist group or to a country that is known to be a base for various terrorist organizations. These trends have not slowed down since, and it is evident that the use of EFTs is a standard practice in the operations of money launderers and terrorist financers.

Finally, since the inception of Canada's EFT reporting regime, 15% of all FINTRAC case disclosures have included only EFTs. Broken down further, 14% of all FINTRAC case disclosures involving money laundering, and 20% of all FINTRAC case disclosures involving terrorist activity financing and other threats to the security of Canada relied exclusively on EFTs.

EFT reports are crucial for making international links between individuals and entities, and establishing patterns indicative of networks that are involved in terrorist activity financing or money laundering activities. For example, the dollar value of EFTs being exchanged between individuals/entities suspected of being involved in such activities can provide insights into the importance of their relationships; the higher the dollar value and the frequency of funds being exchanged, the more significant certain relationships may be.

There is no doubt that collecting EFT data has allowed FINTRAC to considerably expand its capacity to generate meaningful financial intelligence, with relatively little impact on Canada's financial sector. This data has become a key component in the fight against money laundering and terrorist activity financing.

It is imperative that we remain attentive to all current and emerging technologies in our fight against money laundering and terrorist activity financing. FINTRAC can currently track funds that are wired into the U.S. and other countries. If FinCEN and other financial intelligence units are able to collect information on EFTs that cross their borders, it may be possible to track those funds further, perhaps even to their final destinations. Considering the great benefits that this type of reporting has brought to FINTRAC, we are highly supportive of the efforts of other jurisdictions, including the U.S., to implement their own cross-border EFT reporting regimes, as it will certainly aid in broadening the international financial intelligence network.

If you require any further demonstrations on the positive influence that our EFT data collection has had on Canada's AML/CFT regime, we would be pleased to assist you.

I wish you good luck in your pursuit of this initiative.

Sincerely,

Jeanne M. Flemming
Director

Attachment

Swift and Non-Swift reporting requirements, as they are written in the Proceeds of Crime (Money Laundering) and Terrorist Financing Regulations.

SCHEDULE 2

(Paragraphs 12(1)(b) and 28(1)(b) and subsections 52(1), (3) and (4))

OUTGOING SWIFT MESSAGES REPORT INFORMATION

PART A — Transaction Information
1.   Time indication
2.*   Value date
3.*   Amount of electronic funds transfer
4.*   Currency of electronic funds transfer
5.   Exchange rate
6.   Transaction type code

PART B — Information on Client Ordering Payment of Electronic Funds Transfer
1.*   Client's full name
2.*   Client's full address
3.*   Client's account number, if applicable

PART C — Information on Person or Entity Sending Electronic Funds Transfer (person or entity that sends payment instructions)
1.*   (a) Bank Identification Code (BIC)
        - or -
        (b) Full name and full address

PART D — Information on Person or Entity Ordering Electronic Funds Transfer on Behalf of a Client (ordering institution) (if applicable)
1.*   (a) Bank Identification Code (BIC)
        - or -
        (b) Full name and full address

PART E — Information on Sender's Correspondent (person or entity, other than sending person or entity, acting as reimbursement bank for sender) (if applicable)
1.*   (a) Bank Identification Code (BIC)
        - or -
        (b) Full name and full address

PART F — Information on Receiver's Correspondent (person or entity acting as reimbursement bank for receiver) (if applicable)
1.*   (a) Bank Identification Code (BIC)
        - or -
        (b) Full name and full address

PART G — Information on Third Reimbursement Institution (receiver's branch, when the funds are made available to it through a financial institution other than sender's correspondent) (if applicable)

1.*   (a) Bank Identification Code (BIC)

           - or -

           (b) Full name and full address

PART H — Information on Intermediary Institution (financial institution, between receiver and account with institution, through which transaction must pass) (if applicable)

1.*   (a) Bank Identification Code (BIC)

           - or -

           (b) Full name and full address

PART I — Information on Account with Institution (financial institution when other than the receiver that services account for the beneficiary customer) (if applicable)

1.*   (a) Bank Identification Code (BIC)

           - or -

           (b) Full name and full address

PART J — Information on Person or Entity Receiving Electronic Funds Transfer (person or entity receiving payment instructions)

1.*   (a) Bank Identification Code (BIC)

           - or -

           (b) Full name and full address

PART K — Information on Client to Whose Benefit Payment is Made

1.*   Client's full name

2.*   Client's full address

3.*   Client's account number, if applicable

PART L — Additional Payment Information

1.   Remittance information

2.   Details of charges

3.   Sender's charges

4.   Sender's reference

5.   Bank operation code

6.   Instruction code

7.   Sender-to-receiver information

8.   Regulatory reporting

9.   Envelope contents

SCHEDULE 3

(Paragraphs 12(1)(c) and 28(1)(c) and subsections 52(1), (3) and (4))

INCOMING SWIFT MESSAGES REPORT INFORMATION

PART A — Transaction Information
1. Time indication
2.* Value date
3.* Amount of electronic funds transfer
4.* Currency of electronic funds transfer
5. Exchange rate
6. Transaction type code

PART B — Information on Client Ordering Payment of Electronic Funds Transfer
1. Client's full name
2. Client's full address
3. Client's account number, if applicable

PART C — Information on Person or Entity Sending Electronic Funds Transfer (person or entity that sends payment instructions)
1. (a) Bank Identification Code (BIC)
   - or -
   (b) Full name and full address

PART D — Information on Person or Entity Ordering Electronic Funds Transfer on Behalf of a Client (ordering institution)
1. (a) Bank Identification Code (BIC)
   - or -
   (b) Full name and full address

PART E — Information on Sender's Correspondent (person or entity, other than sending person or entity, acting as reimbursement bank for sender) (if applicable)
1. (a) Bank Identification Code (BIC)
   - or -
   (b) Full name and full address

PART F — Information on Receiver's Correspondent (person or entity acting as reimbursement bank for receiver) (if applicable)
1.* (a) Bank Identification Code (BIC)
   - or -
   (b) Full name and full address

PART G — Information on Third Reimbursement Institution (receiver's branch, when the funds are made available to it through a financial institution other than sender's correspondent) (if applicable)
1.* (a) Bank Identification Code (BIC)
   - or -
   (b) Full name and full address

PART H — Information on Intermediary Institution (financial institution, between receiver and account with institution, through which transaction must pass) (if applicable)

    1.*   (a) Bank Identification Code (BIC)

                  - or -

                  (b) Full name and full address

PART I — Information on Account with Institution (financial institution when other than the receiver that services account for the beneficiary customer) (if applicable)

    1.*   (a) Bank Identification Code (BIC)

                  - or -

                  (b) Full name and full address

PART J — Information on Person or Entity Receiving Electronic Funds Transfer (person or entity receiving payment instructions)

    1.*   (a) Bank Identification Code (BIC)

                  - or -

                  (b) Full name and full address

PART K — Information on Client to Whose Benefit Payment is Made

    1.   Client's full name

    2.   Client's full address

    3.   Client's account number, if applicable

PART L — Additional Payment Information

    1.   Remittance information

    2.   Details of charges

    3.   Sender's charges

    4.   Sender's reference

    5.   Bank operation code

    6.   Instruction code

    7.   Sender-to-receiver information

    8.   Regulatory reporting

    9.   Envelope contents

SCHEDULE 5

(Paragraphs 12(1)(b), 28(1)(b) and 40(1)(b) and subsections 52(1) and (3))

OUTGOING NON-SWIFT INTERNATIONAL ELECTRONIC FUNDS TRANSFER REPORT INFORMATION

PART A — Transaction Information
1. Time Sent
2.* Date
3.* Amount of electronic funds transfer
4.* Currency of electronic funds transfer
5. Exchange rate

PART B — Information on Client Ordering Payment of Electronic Funds Transfer
1.* Client's full name
2. Client's full address
3. Client's telephone number
4. Client's date of birth
5. Client's occupation
6.* Client's account number, if applicable
7. Client's identifier
8. Client's Identifier Number

PART C — Information on Sender of Electronic Funds Transfer (person or entity that sends payment instructions)
1.* Full name of sending institution
2.* Full address of sending institution

PART D — Information on Third Party where Client Ordering Electronic Funds Transfer is Acting on Behalf of a Third Party (if applicable)
1. Third party's full name
2. Third party's full address
3. Third party's date of birth
4. Third party's occupation
5. Third party's identifier

PART E — Information on Receiver of Electronic Funds Transfer (person or entity that receives payment instructions)
1. Full name of receiving institution
2. Full address of receiving institution

PART F — Information on Client to Whose Benefit the Payment is Made
1.* Client's full name
2. Client's full address
3. Client's telephone number
4. Client's date of birth
5. Client's occupation
6.* Client's account number, if applicable
7. Client's identifier

5

PART G — Information on Third Party where Client to Whose Benefit Payment is Made is Acting on Behalf of a Third Party (if applicable)

    1.   Third party's full name
    2.   Third party's full address
    3.   Third party's date of birth
    4.   Third party's occupation
    5.   Third party's identifier

SCHEDULE 6

(Paragraphs 12(1)(c), 28(1)(c) and 40(1)(c) and subsections 52(1) and (3))

INCOMING NON-SWIFT INTERNATIONAL ELECTRONIC FUNDS TRANSFER REPORT INFORMATION

PART A — Transaction Information

    1.   Time sent
    2.*   Date
    3.*   Amount of electronic funds transfer
    4.*   Currency of electronic funds transfer
    5.   Exchange rate

PART B — Information on Client Ordering Payment of an Electronic Funds Transfer

    1.*   Client's full name
    2.   Client's full address
    3.   Client's telephone number
    4.   Client's date of birth
    5.   Client's occupation
    6.*   Client's account number, if applicable
    7.   Client's identifier
    8.   Client's Identifier Number

PART C — Information on Sender of Electronic Funds Transfer (person or entity that sends payment instructions)

    1.*   Full name of sending institution
    2.*   Full address of sending institution

PART D — Information on Third Party where Client Ordering Electronic Funds Transfer is Acting on Behalf of a Third Party (if applicable)

    1.   Third party's full name
    2.   Third party's full address
    3.   Third party's date of birth
    4.   Third party's occupation
    5.   Third party's identifier

PART E — Information on Receiver of Electronic Funds Transfer (person or entity that receives payment instructions)

1.*   Full name of receiving institution
2.*   Full address of receiving institution

PART F — Information on Client to Whose Benefit the Payment is Made

1.*   Client's full name
2.   Client's full address
3.   Client's telephone number
4.   Client's date of birth
5.   Client's occupation
6.*   Client's account number, if applicable
7.   Client's identifier

PART G — Information on Third Party where Client to Whose Benefit Payment is Made is Acting on Behalf of a Third Party (if applicable)

1.   Third party's full name
2.   Third party's full address
3.   Third party's date of birth
4.   Third party's occupation
5.   Third party's identifier

**REPUBLIC OF CROATIA
MINISTRY OF FINANCE
ANTI-MONEY LAUNDERING
OFFICE**

Ref.: 470-06/08-02/5
        513-06-1/023-2
Zagreb, 28/02/2008

> **U.S. DEPARTMENT OF TREASURY
> FINCEN
> Attn. Mr. James H. Freis, Director**

LETTER OF SUPPORT

Dear Mr. Freis,

Croatian Anti-Money Laundering Office (Croatian FIU) has learned about FinCEN's efforts to further develop its analytical and risk-based approach targeted to cross-border wire transfers through collection of certain international wire transfers from financial institutions such as banks and money transmitters and to use it to safeguard the financial system from the abuses of financial crime, including terrorist financing, money laundering, and other illicit activities.

In Croatia, there are existing regimes of cross-border wire transfers data collection in relation to some macroeconomic analysis, specific ways of cross-border financial control, and the FIU work.

The Croatian National Bank gathers data related to external operations that do not represent single transactions i.e. electronic transfers although they refer to international transactions (except for the part of external payment operations).

For the purpose of the statistics on external operations (balance of payment statistics, international investment position and external debt) the Croatian National

Bank currently implements following statistical researches (some are available on web):

International transactions related to construction services
International transportation services
International transactions related to communication services
International transactions related to insurance services
Foreign direct and portfolio investments, credit operations and deposit resident transactions abroad
Transactions related to real estates and land trading
External payment operations

Since gathered data are used primarily for the purpose of compiling balance of payment, all information on transactions included in the payment order are not being gathered but only some of characteristics. Those data are used by the Croatian National Bank, in charge to compile balance of payment, as well as the Foreign Exchange Inspectorate responsible for foreign exchange supervision (including AML related supervision). The threshold for reporting will be introduced in the future (by harmonizing with the *acquis communautaire* of the EU).

Regarding the cross-border wire transfers data received by the FIU it can be stated that till 2003 two types of suspicious transaction reports (STRs) have been received:
- STRs according to the "subjective indicators" (suspicious transactions related to criminal activity; large, complex transaction without economic purpose etc., suspicious cross-border wire transfers included) irrespective of the amount,
- STRs according to the "objective indicators" (all transactions from/to offshore, NCCTs, terrorism related countries; all cross-border wire transfers over 100.000 USD)
First group is used for initiating the cases while the second group was used primarily as additional database; for initiating cases regarding some specific patterns recognized (frequency etc.), and for statistical and analytical purposes (specific types of transactions, countries related etc.). Although the second type filled the FIU database with significant amount of transactions, since 2003 those "objective indicators" have been suspended including all further cross-border wire transfers over 100.000 USD (except suspicious). Today, only STR related regime is valid (and STR related cross-border wire transfers).

Taking into account Croatian size (population, number of AML obliged entities with 34 banks, volume of international transactions) and definitively ML/FT risks that Croatia is exposed or not exposed to, Croatian FIU concluded that this approach is not essential for our circumstances.

However, systematic and continuous analysis of comprehensive cross-border wire transfers data base could result with, not only important additional further data on cases investigated and some statistical indicators, but also with: data needed for full implementation of FATF Recommendation 11, specific patterns and trends could be identified, indicators for recognizing suspicious transactions further developed, and preventive measures focused on assessed and recognized risk areas.

As mentioned above, taking into account Croatian size and definitively assessed ML/TF risks that Croatia is exposed to, Croatian FIU concluded that this approach (all cross-border wire transfers data) is not essential for our circumstances and focuses its work on STRs, and STRs related strategic analysis. With recent organizational changes of the FIU, new FIU Informational System and Strategic Analysis Department has been established. Except available data on STRs, CTRs, Customs reports, and opened cases, it is foreseen that other, internationally available data should be used in providing strategic analysis, providing reports on trends, patterns, threats, and indicators. International experience is going to be added value and cooperation with FinCEN in that field very important.

Taking all mentioned into account, Croatian FIU respects and fully supports the idea of introducing the cross-border wire transfers data collection approach of the FinCEN as proper way of developing and strengthening AML/CFT preventive regime, recognizing possible threats and timely reacting in the effective way.

Yours sincerely,

Mr. Ivica Maros
Director of the AMLO

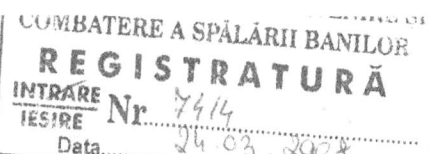

ROMANIAN GOVERNMENT
NATIONAL OFFICE FOR PREVENTION
AND CONTROL OF MONEY LAUNDERING
1, Ion Florescu Street, Sector 3, Bucharest, Romania
Phone: 00-4021-315.52.07, 00-4021-315.52.80
Fax: 00-4021-315.52.27, E-mail: onpcsb@onpcsb.ro
Web site: www.onpcsb.ro

FINANCIAL CRIMES ENFORCEMENT NETWORK, US DEPARTMENT OF TREASURY

To the kind attention of Mr. JAMES H. FREIS Jr., Director

Dear Mr. Freis,

We received with great interest the letter sent on December 27, 2007, by the Financial Crimes Enforcement Network (FINCEN), the Financial Intelligence Unit of the United States of America, regarding the development of a project for highlighting the benefits and the value added of the wire transfers (hereinafter called cross-border) called reports submitted by the financial institutions to the FIU.

In the spirit of a good professional relationships between the Financial Intelligence Units from USA and Romania, the National Office for Prevention and Control of Money Laundering expressed its full availability and interest in implementing this project, as communicated in our letter sent on December 28, 2007.

In this context and having in mind the details of the project kindly disseminated by Mr. Andrew Shankman, Project Administrator, on behalf of FINCEN – SUA, we would like to present to you the main aspects, with reference to the method of reporting and the use of cross-border transfers, as follows:

I. Legal Framework:

According to art. 19 of the Law no. 656/2002 on prevention and sanctioning money laundering and on setting up of certain measures for the prevention and combating terrorism financing, with the subsequent amendments and completions (hereinafter called the Law no. 656/2002), the National Office for Prevention and Control of Money Laundering (NOPCML) functions as a specialized body having legal personality, subordinated to the Government of Romania, and in coordination of the Prime Minister Chancellery, having the object of activity the prevention and combating money laundering and terrorist financing, in which purposes it receives, analyses and processes information and notifies, when solid grounds of money laundering or financing of terrorist activities exist, the General Prosecution's Office by the High Court of Cassation and Justice and, in case of suspicions regarding transactions connected with terrorism financing, the General Prosecution's Office by the High Court of Cassation and Justice and the Romanian Intelligence Service.

According to the provisions of art. 3 para. 7 of the Law no. 656/2002, the natural and legal persons that are subject of the AML/CTF Law (hereinafter called reporting entities) have the obligation to report to the NOPCML, within 24 hours, the cross-border transfers in and from accounts for amounts of money whose minimum limit is the equivalent in RON (national currency) of 10,000 EUR.

We mention that the law defines at art. 2 letter d) *"the cross-border transfers in and from accounts"* as being *"payments and withdrawals performed between persons from the Romanian territory and persons situated abroad"*.

Also, according to art. 3 para. 1 the Law 656/2002, the reporting entities are obliged to fill in Suspicious Transaction Reports (STRs), as soon as there are suspicions that a transaction, which is to be performed, has the purpose of money laundering or terrorism financing.

These suspicious transactions could include[1] *"external transfers or other operations that do not seem to be of an economical, commercial or legal nature, including external transfers that do not fall within the statutory activity of the customer or that are requested by customers not engaged in this statutory activity"*, as well.

In these situations, the reporting entities will be obliged to fill in a STR, notwithstanding the amount involved in these transactions.

The form and content of the three types of reports received by NOPCML, namely the Suspicious Transaction Report, the Cash Transaction Reports for amounts in RON or foreign currency whose minimum limit represents the equivalent in RON of 10,000 EUR, indifferent if the transaction is performed through one or several linked operations and the Cross-border Report in and from accounts for amounts of money whose minimum limit is the equivalent in RON of 10,000 EUR, have been settled by the NOPCML's Board by Decision no. 276/16.06.2005, published in the Official Gazette no. 558/29.06.2005.

II.   The reporting, the access and using method of the data regarding cross-border transfers.

The reports on cross-border transfers in and from accounts for amounts of money whose minimum limit is the equivalent in RON of 10,000 EUR are filled in by the credit institutions and are transmitted to the National Office for Prevention and Control of Money Laundering, electronically or on-line, through the inter-banking secured network.

The report contains information on the operation, the customer of the reporting entity, the legal representative of the customer, the person empowered by the client to perform the transaction, the foreign bank, the foreign bank's customer.

---

[1] According to art. 42 para. 2 letter c) from the Norms of National Bank of Romania no. 3 /26.02.2002 on know your customer standards, with the subsequent amendments and completions.

These reports are loaded on daily basis within a special database held by the NOPCML, especially created only for the internal access of the institution.

The information from this database can be accessed by the members of the NOPCML' Board, financial analysts and assistants within the institution, for:

- ✓ capitalisation of information in the financial analysis,
- ✓ performing the on-site and off-site supervision,
- ✓ performing checks within the procedure of information exchange between the NOPCML and foreign institutions having similar attributions;
- ✓ elaboration of statistical data, used for the drafting the annual report as well, for ensuring a general feedback of the NOPCML to the reporting entities and to the authorities of financial control and prudential supervision.

The Suspicious Transaction Reports (STRs) are transmitted by the reporting entities to the Office, on paper and electronic format, in an encrypted file.

The STRs are loaded on daily basis, in a special database of the NOPCML, this database being the starting point for each analysis performed by the financial analysts.

On this occasion, we would like to mention the NOPCML does not perform automatic financial analyses on the cross-border transfers in and from accounts for amounts of money whose minimum limit is the equivalent in RON of 10,000 EUR, the information from the database being used by the specialized directorate as long as it refers to a financial flow linked with the analysed suspicious transactions.

On the same time, in accordance with art. 17 para (1) letter b) of the Law 656/2002 *"for the persons which are not are under supervision of any authority, according to the regulations in force, the supervision, checking and control attributions shall be fulfilled by the Office".*

For the fulfilment of this attribution, the Board of the NOPCML issued the **Decision no. 496/11.07.2006 for the approval of the Norms on prevention and combating money laundering and terrorism financing, customer due diligence and internal control standards for reporting entities, which do not have overseeing authorities, published in the Official Gazette no. 623/19.07.2006.**

Since the beginning of 2007, the NOPCML also issued the **Working procedures on supervision, verification and control activities developed to the natural/legal persons provided in the art.8 (reporting entities) of the Law no.656/2002.**

The specialized department, during the verifying and control actions performed at the headquarters of the reporting entities – the on-site supervision – gathers data and information regarding the cross-border transfers in and from accounts for amounts of money whose minimum limit is the equivalent in RON of 10,000 EUR, which are subsequently analysed in comparison with the results of the applications used within the off-site supervision.

III. International Cooperation

Based on the provisions of art. 5 para 4 from the Law no. 656/2002 according to which *„the Office may exchange information, based on reciprocity, with foreign institutions having similar functions and which are equally obliged to keeping secrecy, if such information exchange is made with the purpose of preventing and combating money laundering and terrorism financing"*, **the exchange of information between the NOPCML and other FIUs is made operatively through two secured IT systems offered by the Egmont Group and FIU.NET.**

The exchange of information between the NOPCML and the foreign Financial Intelligence Units is performed in accordance with the national legal provisions, indicated above, and with respect to the **" Best Practices for exchange of information between the Financial Intelligence Units"** issued by the Egmont Group, the international organization NOPCML is member of, starting from May 2000.

In this context, we would like to present the following the aspects evidencing the need of cooperation in the information exchange field, in particular, on obtaining data and information related to cross-border transfers:

- the requests of information are transmitted from/to the NOPCML, based on external elements, which are, in the majority of cases, generated by the existence of cross-border transfers in/from Romania;
- by the requests of information, data and information are transmitted, in order to:
  - identify the source and legal or illegal origin of the funds,
  - identify the beneficial owner of transactions and the economic justification,
  - make the existing connections with the involved persons,
  - gather information necessary for confirming/denying the existence of serious grounds for ML and TF.
- by the requests of information can be asked for identification of the predicate offence generating dirty money, which is the basis of the activities of ML/TF performed on the Romanian territory;
- the requests of information are transmitted with priority, in cases when there is a need of verifying the link between the persons being analysed based on possible activities of financing terrorism;
- by the requests of information can be detected the financial international flow, as well as the commercial one;
- by the requests including information on eventual external activities of money laundering or terrorism financing, it may be asked the suspension of transaction by the FIU and taking the appropriate measures by the law enforcement authorities.

IV. Statistical data on cross-border transfers

In accordance with the provisions of art. 6 para. 7 of the Law no. 656/2002, the Office provides "to the natural and legal persons under art. 8[2], as well as to the financial control and prudential supervision authorities, by an adequate procedure, general information about the suspicious transactions and typologies of money laundering and terrorism financing", ensuring, in this way, delivering of a general feedback on the situation of reports and notifications submitted to the institution.

In this context, we would like to present below the following statistical data on the reports transfers in and from accounts for amounts of money whose minimum limit is the equivalent in RON of 10,000 EUR, registered during the period 2003-2007, data which have been included in the annual reports on the NOPCML activity:

Years	Total of reports	Total of transfers	No. of transfers in Romania	No. of transfers from Romania	No. of operations performed by natural persons	No. of operations performed by legal persons	Total amounts (mil. Euro)	Amounts in Romania (mil. Euro)	Amounts out of Romania (mil. Euro)
2003	7.301	496.438	198.190	298.248	11.878	183.311	28.479	13064	15.415
2004	8.981	756.205	473.983	282.222	33.372	722.833	47.254	24.473	22.781
2005	8.761	1.008.871	380.601	628.270	49.616	959.255	90.552	41.105	49.447
2006	8.886	1.192.930	434.859	758.071	61.948	1.130.982	184.532	95.313	89.219
2007	8.702	1.469.740	507.920	961.820	93.332	1.376.408	173.805	86.512	87.293

Hoping that the information provided by the National Office for Prevention and Control of Money Laundering offered a clear overview of the modality of use of data included in the reports transfers in and from accounts for amounts of money whose minimum limit is the equivalent in RON of 10,000 EUR, in the activity of the Financial Intelligence Unit, please do not hesitate to contact us for obtaining any additional information.

Kindest regards,

ADRIANA LUMINITA POPA

President
National Office for Prevention and
Control of Money Laundering

---

[2] Reporting Entities

Appendix C: Survey & CFI Survey Results

(Survey and Survey Results Follow)

FinCEN
Department of the Treasury

2008 Cross-Border Electronic Funds Transfer Survey

Final Report
March 2008

FCG

American Customer
Satisfaction Index

This page intentionally left blank.

TABLE OF CONTENTS

This page intentionally left blank.

Introduction

In order to evaluate the cost and impact that a proposed cross-border electronic funds transmittal reporting requirement would have, CFI Group was contracted by FinCEN through the Federal Consulting Group (FCG) to conduct a survey. CFI Group surveyed those organizations that would be directly affected by this proposed requirement, depository institutions and money transmitters. In the survey, respondents were presented with the specifications of the proposed requirement and then asked a series of questions about the impact the requirement would have on their operations, costs, and potential benefits. The findings are provided in this report. The questionnaire that was used for the study can be found in Appendix A. The following passage from the introduction of the survey explains in detail the background that necessitated the study and the following report.

Section 6302 of the Intelligence Reform and Terrorism Prevention Act of 2004 (Act) requires, among other things, that the Secretary of the Treasury study the feasibility of "requiring such financial institutions as the Secretary determines to be appropriate to report to the Financial Crimes Enforcement Network (FinCEN) certain cross-border electronic transmittals of funds, if the Secretary determines that reporting of such transmittals is reasonably necessary to conduct the efforts of the Secretary against money laundering and terrorist financing." Prior to prescribing any such regulations, however, the Secretary must report to Congress regarding what cross-border information would be reasonably necessary to combat money laundering and terrorist financing; outline the criteria to be used in determining what situations require reporting; outline the form, manner, and frequency of reporting; and identify the technology necessary for FinCEN to keep, analyze, protect, and disseminate the data collected.

To meet these requirements, FinCEN completed a study that assessed the overall feasibility of establishing a limited cross-border funds transmittal reporting requirement for certain financial institutions. FinCEN reported the results of that study to Congress in October 2006. The report concluded that while it may be feasible to establish a limited cross-border funds transmittal reporting requirement on certain financial institutions, it would require additional time and resources to identify and would require a cost-benefit analysis to determine if it would be appropriate to implement a reporting regime. The report also provided general responses regarding FinCEN's administrative approach and needed data security measures to support any data reporting. The report also concluded that the basic information already obtained and maintained by U.S. financial institutions (banks and non-bank financial institutions) pursuant to the Funds Transfer Rule, including the $3,000 recordkeeping threshold, provides sufficient basis for meaningful data analysis. In addition, any reporting requirement should apply only to those U.S. institutions that exchange payment instructions directly with foreign institutions. Finally, the $3,000 recordkeeping threshold should apply only to discrete transactions and not to the aggregated total value of multiple transactions conducted very closely to one another in time.

To better understand the implications for the U.S. financial services industry and the government the report recommended proceeding further on an incremental basis to validate the continued appropriateness of any reporting requirement. To that end, FinCEN is identifying and quantifying the potential benefits and costs of any potential cross-border funds transmittal reporting requirement. To determine the benefit to U.S. anti-money laundering and counter-terrorist financing activities, FinCEN is engaging law enforcement, regulatory, and intelligence communities to identify and quantify the value of the potential data reporting. FinCEN is also evaluating its ability to manage, protect, and analyze any reported data and the associated costs and benefits. For the costs to the financial services industry, economy, and payments system, FinCEN is engaging with the industry and key regulatory and payment system participants, including via this survey.

Executive Summary

➢ Identification of which transfers and transmittals would be reportable under the new requirements is not an issue for depository institutions or money transmitters. Respondents almost uniformly said they would be able to identify transmittals that would need to be reported to FinCEN under the proposed requirement – 89% of depository institution respondents and all money transmitter respondents replied they would be able to identify payments that needed to be reported.

➢ Collectively, it is estimated from survey data that depository institutions (i.e. domestic and foreign SWIFT banks) accounted for approximately 1.1 billion to 1.6 billion transmittals in 2006 with U.S. SWIFT banks accounting for approximately one billion of those.

➢ On average the largest SWIFT banks (i.e. those with assets over $1 billion) reported for the year 2006 having over 1.3 million transactions that would have been considered reportable. For smaller banks (i.e. those with assets of $1billion or less) the average number of transactions is a fraction of that (just over 6 thousand). It is estimated that in 2006 domestic SWIFT banks collectively had approximately 143 million transactions that could be considered reportable. For foreign SWIFT banks it is estimated between 81 million and 137 million of such transactions occurred in 2006.

   o Overall, respondents expect a 27% increase in the number of reportable transactions in 2010 compared to the number of 2006 transactions. Thus, for 2010 it is estimated that domestic SWIFT banks would conduct approximately 182 million transactions that would be reportable. For foreign SWIFT banks the estimate for 2010 ranges from 103 million to 147 million.

➢ With respect to transactions that are under $3,000 but would otherwise have been reportable, it appears that foreign SWIFT banks would conduct more of these types of transactions than U.S. SWIFT banks. The estimate for U.S.SWIFT banks is approximately 90 million in total, but for all foreign SWIFT banks the total number of these types of transactions ranges from 120 to 170 million.

➢ Respondents expected an increase in cost associated with complying with the new reporting requirement compared to the cost of responding to subpoenas or other legal demands. The largest U.S. SWIFT banks expect an average cost of implementation on the order of one-quarter million dollars and an annual expense on average in excess of 80 thousand dollars. Foreign SWIFT banks on average, expect much lower costs for implementation – just over 50 thousand dollars and annual costs on the order of approximately 60 thousand dollars.

   o The total implementation costs for the proposed requirement to all domestic SWIFT banks ranges from approximately $13 million to $28 million. In addition to the implementation costs, there are annual costs associated with the reporting requirement. These total to a range of approximately $5 to $12 million dollars annually for domestic banks. The total implementation costs to all foreign SWIFT banks would range from approximately just under $4 million to just over $5 million. The total annual costs to all foreign SWIFT banks could be greater than implementation costs with a range of approximately $2 million to $6 million.

➢ For money transmitters, there are not enough data points to extrapolate to the entire population, however one of the responses collected was among the 6 largest money transmitters (those with over 100,000 branches). They estimated the implementation cost to be approximately $250,000 and the annual costs to be just over $50,000. *Assuming these costs are representative of the 6 money transmitters of this size, the total implementation costs would be approximate 1.5 million and the total annual costs to the (6) largest money transmitters would be approximately $300 thousand.*

➢ With respect to annual costs, personnel and on-going management account for nearly two-thirds of estimated annual costs overall. For implementation costs, software development, systems upgrades and programming collectively account for nearly half of the costs.

➤ Respondents do not expect a decrease in the volume, value or quality of transmittals as a result of the new reporting requirement. Thus, it can be inferred the 27% increase in the number of transmittals from 2006 to 2010 reported by respondents is likely expected due to growth in business.

Data Collection

Sample

Data were collected via e-mail and fax from January 4, 2008 through February 15, 2008. FinCEN supplied CFI Group with a list of contacts to be surveyed. These included depository institutions, of which there were a total of 147 domestic banks and 100 foreign banks. In addition to depository institutions, 32 money transmitters were included in the sample. *Depository institutions are defined as all depository institution members of the Society for Worldwide Interbank Financial Telecommunications (SWIFT) user group located or doing business in the United States, including offices or agents of non-U.S. chartered depository institutions. Money transmitters are defined as all nonbank financial institutions that were registered with FinCEN as a "Money Transmitter" on November 10, 2007 and reported at least one branch location in the United States.*

The tables below provide a breakdown of the three main types of organizations that were included in the study: domestic banks, foreign banks and money transmitters. Organizations are stratified by assets or in the case of money transmitters by number of branches. For banking institutions the entire population of SWIFT banks was provided in the sample. For money transmitters, a small portion of the population was provided as a sample.

For U.S. banks, i.e. U.S. SWIFT banks with a U.S. location, over two-thirds (69%) of the banks in the sample have assets of over $1 billion. These institutions are classified as stratum 1 banks. Another 18% of the U.S. banks were known to have assets between $100 million and $1 billion (classified as stratum 2) and 5% of the U.S. banks had assets under $100 million (classified as stratum 3). There were a small number of U.S. banks (7%) where the assets were unknown or undefined. This group is represented as stratum 4.

Figure 1: Population of Domestic Banks

All U.S. SWIFT banks with a U.S. location by strata (assets)	Total Population	Percentage of total
Stratum 1 (Assets > $1 billion)	102	69%
Stratum 2 (Assets $100M to $1B)	27	18%
Stratum 3 (Assets < $100M)	7	5%
Stratum 4 (Assets undefined)	11	7%

Most foreign banks do not report data to the FDIC and no information about their total assets is available. This includes 80% of the foreign banks, i.e. foreign SWIFT banks with a U.S. location. For those few foreign banks where data on assets exist, 8% have assets over $1 billion (stratum 1). Eleven percent have assets between $100 million and $1 billion (stratum 2) and one bank was known to have assets under $100 million (stratum 3). For both foreign and domestic banks, the sample provided by FinCEN was the population. However, the data on assets for four-fifths of the foreign SWIFT banks are unknown. These organizations are classified as stratum 4.

Figure 2: Population of Foreign Banks

All Foreign SWIFT banks with a U.S. location by strata (assets)	Total Population	Percentage of total
Stratum 1 (Assets > $1 billion)	8	8%
Stratum 2 (Assets $100M to $1B)	11	11%
Stratum 3 (Assets < $100M)	1	1%
Stratum 4 (Assets undefined)	80	80%

Only a small sample of contact information for money transmitters was available for the survey. The total sample of money transmitters included 32 contacts. The breakdown by strata as defined by number of branches is given below. Given the small sample and small number of responses from money transmitters reporting for this group is somewhat limited.

Figure 3: Sample and Population of Money Transmitters

Registered money transmitters by strata (branches)	Total Population	Survey Sample Size
Stratum 1 (100,000+ branches)	6	2
Stratum 2 (100 to 100,000 branches)	67	13
Stratum 3 (1 to 99 branches)	8,054	17

Responses

Summing the sample of domestic SWIFT banks, foreign SWIFT banks and money transmitters yields a total of 279 potential respondents. Among these groups a total of 81 responses were collected for a 29% response rate. This is a relatively high response rate given the significant time commitment required for the survey (estimated at 2 hours). Of the 81 responses collected, 35 were collected from domestic SWIFT banks, 40 were collected from foreign SWIFT banks and 6 were collected from money transmitters. Foreign SWIFT banks had the highest rate of response (40%), followed by domestic SWIFT banks (29%) and money transmitters (19%).

The responses received from domestic SWIFT banks were representative of the population with respect to their assets. In both the overall sample and among those who had responded, 69% had assets of over $1 billion. Thus responses from the largest institutions were proportionate to both their population in the sample and to the universe of domestic SWIFT banks.

Figure 4: Domestic Banks Responses

Domestic Bank Responses	Number of responses	Percentage of domestic responses
Stratum 1 (Assets > $1 billion)	24	69%
Stratum 2 (Assets $100M to $1B)	5	14%
Stratum 3 (Assets < $100M)	1	3%
Stratum 4 (Assets undefined)	5	14%

Given that a majority of foreign SWIFT banks report no figures for assets to the FDIC, very few of the responses from foreign SWIFT banks have asset data associated with them. Only 7 of the 40 foreign SWIFT bank respondents do have asset data associated with them. For purposes of analysis in this report, where appropriate, banks will be grouped by strata regardless of domestic or foreign status.

Figure 5: Foreign Banks Responses

Foreign Bank Responses	Number of responses	Percentage of foreign bank responses
Stratum 1 (Assets > $1 billion)	3	7.5%
Stratum 2 (Assets $100M to $1B)	4	10%
Stratum 3 (Assets < $100M)	0	0%
Stratum 4 (Assets undefined)	33	82.5%

Only 6 money transmitters responded to the survey. Of these, 4 had fewer than 100 branches, one had more than 1,000 but fewer than 100,000 branches and one had more than 100,000 branches.

Figure 6: Money Transmitters Responses

Registered money transmitters by strata (branches)	Number of responses
Stratum 1 (100,000+ branches)	1
Stratum 2 (100 to 100,000 branches)	1
Stratum 3 (1 to 99 branches)	4

Respondent Location

The figure below provides the geographic region of the U.S. branch from where the respondent was located. Nearly half of the respondents were located in the Northeast and one-quarter of the respondents were from the West. A total of 16 states were represented by the location of institutions' headquarters. However, the states of New York and California accounted for 69% of respondents.

Figure 7: Location of respondent

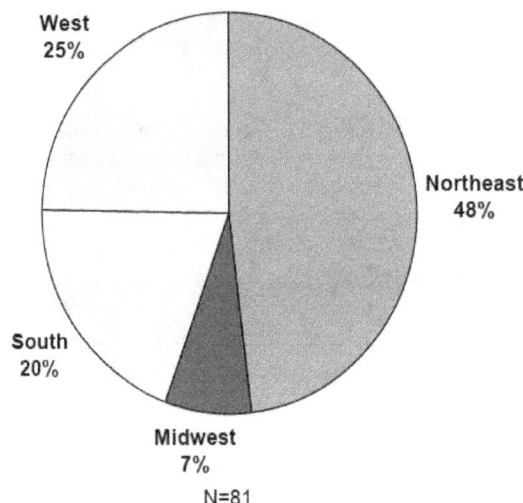

N=81

The Northeast region includes: Connecticut, Maine, Massachusetts, New Hampshire, New Jersey, New York, Rhode Island, Pennsylvania and Vermont. The Midwest region includes: Illinois, Indiana, Iowa, Kansas, Michigan, Minnesota, Missouri, Nebraska, North Dakota, Ohio, South Dakota and Wisconsin. The South region includes: Alabama, Arkansas, Delaware, District of Columbia, Florida, Georgia, Kentucky, Louisiana, Maryland, Mississippi, North Carolina, Oklahoma, South Carolina, Tennessee, Texas, Virginia and West Virginia. The West region includes: Alaska, Arizona, California, Colorado, Hawaii, Idaho, Montana, Nevada, New Mexico, Oregon, Utah, Washington and Wyoming.

Key Findings

Identifying payments or transmittals that would need to be reported

Respondents were asked based on the description of potentially reportable cross-border electronic funds transfer/transmittals would their institutions be able to identify the payment or transmittal orders that would need to be reported to FinCEN. This did not seem to be an issue for a majority of respondents.

All of the money transmitters surveyed (sample of 6) and 89% of depository institutions that responded claimed they would be able to identify the payments that would need to be reported to FinCEN. Among depository institutions there was a small, but not a significant difference between foreign SWIFT banks (92.5%) and domestic SWIFT banks (86%) being able to identify the payments or transmittal orders that would need to be reported to FinCEN.

Number of electronic funds transmittals processed in 2006 and estimates for 2010

Respondents were asked about (1) the total number of electronic funds processed in 2006 that would have been considered reportable, (2) the number of transmittals processed in 2006 that were under $3,000 that would have otherwise met the requirements and been considered reportable and (3) the estimated number of transactions in 2010 that could be considered reportable. The following section reports on all three items and compares responses from questions (1) and (3) to illustrate the change in the number of reportable transactions from 2006 to the expected number in 2010.

Note: The tables below group banks by strata regardless of domestic or foreign status.

Among Stratum 1 banks, (which also includes responses from foreign banks known to have assets over $1 billion), the mean number of transactions conducted in 2006 that would have been considered reportable was 1.365 million. There was a great range among respondents, even within each stratum group, as to the number of transactions. This range is also reflected by the difference between average and median numbers shown in the table below. However, smaller banks on average had very few reportable transactions.

Figure 8: Average and median number of transactions processed in 2006 that would have been considered reportable

	Banks Stratum 1 (Assets over $1B)	Banks Strata 2 and 3 (Assets $1B and under)	Banks Stratum 4 (Assets unknown)	Money Transmitters
Average number of transactions	1,365,940	6,171	257,866	65,357
Median number of transactions	41,188	83	1,408	3,772
N	26	10	37	6

Figure 9: Reportable Transactions for Bank Stratum 1 (Assets over $1 Billion)

Total number of transactions processed that could be considered reportable	Number of institutions in category for 2006	Number of institutions in category for 2010 estimate
1,000,000 or more	5	7
100,000 to 999,999	5	3
50,000 to 99,999	3	2
1,000 to 49,999	6	4
1 to 999	4	4
0	3	3

The table shows the breakdown of institutions by number of transactions. Five banks had over 1 million transactions in 2006 that could be considered reportable and there were five banks between 100,000 and

999,999. Nine banks had between 1,000 and 99,999 and seven banks reported less than 1,000 transactions that would be in this category.

Regardless of the number of transactions an institution claimed were reportable in 2006, most estimated that the number of reportable transaction would go up significantly from 2006 to 2010 with the mean score for number of reportable transactions for 2010 at 2 million.

There were only 10 banks that had known assets under $1 billion. Overall, this group reported much lower numbers of transactions that the stratum 1 banks reported. On average 6,852 transactions would have been reportable in 2006 among this group. For 2010, that number is estimated to increase to 9,282.

Figure 10: Reportable Transactions for Bank Strata 2 and 3 (Assets $1 Billion and under)

Total number of transactions processed that could be considered reportable	Number of institutions in category for 2006	Number of institutions in category for 2010 estimate
50,000 to 99,999	0	1
1,000 to 49,999	4	3
1 to 999	4	4
0	2	2

Most of the foreign banks and a few of the domestic banks fall into the category of unknown assets. Of these, the average number of reportable transactions in 2006 was just over one-quarter million (257,866).

Only one of the stratum 4 banks had over 1,000,000 reportable transactions in 2006 and only six had at least 100,000, while 17 had fewer than 1,000 reportable transactions. As was found with the other groups, the number of reportable transactions is expected to increase in 2010. Of those with at least 1,000 reportable transactions in 2006, on average a 20% increase in the number of reportable transactions was expected for 2010.

Figure 11: Reportable Transactions for Bank Stratum 4 (Assets unknown)

Total number of transactions processed that could be considered reportable	Number of institutions in category for 2006	Number of institutions in category for 2010 estimate
1,000,000 or more	1	1
100,000 to 999,999	5	4
50,000 to 99,999	2	3
1,000 to 49,999	12	14
1 to 999	11	12
0	6	3

A total of six money transmitters responded to the survey. On average, they had 65,357 reportable transactions in 2006. Only three money transmitters that responded expected reportable transactions in both 2006 and 2010 on average a 22% increase in the number of transactions was expected.

Figure 12: Reportable Transactions for Money Transmitters

Total number of transactions processed that could be considered reportable	Number of institutions in category for 2006	Number of institutions in category for 2010 estimate
100,000 to 999,999	1	1
50,000 to 99,999	0	0
1,000 to 49,999	2	2
1 to 999	1	0
0	2	3

In sum, while there is great variance in the number of transmittals across all groups, most expect an increase in reportable transmittals. Across all respondents the average expected increase for 2010 is approximately 27% higher than the 2006 figure*.

*This figure (27%) was derived from regression analysis of responses to Q1i (independent variable) and Q1iii (dependent variable). The coefficient of the equation was 1.273 indicating an expected increase of 27.3%. The model equation has an adjusted R-squared of .985.

Figure 13: Average and median number of transactions processed in 2006 that would have been considered reportable compared to 2010 estimates

	Banks Stratum 1 (Assets over $1B)	Banks Strata 2 and 3 (Assets $1B and under)	Banks Stratum 4 (Assets unknown)	Money Transmitters
Average number of transactions - 2006	1,365,940	6,171	257,866	65,357
Average number of transactions - 2010	2,024,451	8,360	303,165	90,151
Percent increase	48%	35%	18%	38%
Median number of transactions - 2006	41,188	83	1,408	3,772
Median number of transactions - 2010	45,262	90	2,063	4,000
Percent increase	10%	9%	47%	6%
N	24	10	37	6

Transmittals processed in 2006 that were under $3,000 that would have otherwise met the requirements and been considered reportable

Respondents were asked about the transmittals that were processed in 2006 that were under $3,000 and would have otherwise met the requirements to be considered reportable. For the largest banks (i.e. assets over $1 Billion), the average number is just over 700 thousand transmittals. For smaller banks (i.e. assets $1 Billion and under) the average is just over two thousand. Although the sample of money transmitters is quite small, those in this group who were surveyed had a considerable number of transmittals under $3,000 that would otherwise met requirements. The average for this group was over 900 thousand transmittals.

Figure 14: Average and median number of transmittals processed in 2006 that were under $3,000 that would have otherwise met the requirements and been considered reportable

	Banks Stratum 1 (Assets over $1B)	Banks Strata 2 and 3 (Assets $1B and under)	Banks Stratum 4 (Assets unknown)	Money Transmitters
Average number of transactions	704,133	2,290	1,717,588	8,462,901
Median number of transactions	10,550	144	2,639	915,245
N	24	10	35	6

The following tables provide a further breakdown of the number of transmittals by strata and organization type for transactions under $3,000.

Figure 15: Transactions under $3,000 otherwise reportable for Bank Stratum 1 (Assets over $1 Billion)

Total number of transmittals processed that were under $3,000 that would have otherwise met the requirements and been considered reportable	Number of institutions in category for 2006
1,000,000 or more	5
100,000 to 999,999	2
50,000 to 99,999	2
1,000 to 49,999	7
1 to 999	5
0	3

Figure 16: Transactions under $3,000 otherwise reportable for Bank Strata 2 and 3 (Assets $1 Billion and under)

Total number of transmittals processed that were under $3,000 that would have otherwise met the requirements and been considered reportable	Number of institutions in category for 2006
1,000 to 49,999	2
1 to 999	5
0	3

Figure 17: Transactions under $3,000 otherwise reportable for Bank Stratum 4 (Assets unknown)

Total number of transmittals processed that were under $3,000 that would have otherwise met the requirements and been considered reportable	Number of institutions in category for 2006
1,000,000 or more	1
100,000 to 999,999	1
50,000 to 99,999	1
1,000 to 49,999	14
1 to 999	13
0	5

Figure 18: Transactions under $3,000 otherwise reportable for Money Transmitters

Total number of transmittals processed that were under $3,000 that would have otherwise met the requirements and been considered reportable	Number of institutions in category for 2006
1,000,000 or more	3
100,000 to 999,999	1
50,000 to 99,999	0
1,000 to 49,999	0
1 to 999	0
0	2

Computing total number of transactions

Respondents provided the total number of transactions processed in 2006 that could be considered reportable and also gave this figure as a percentage of all electronic funds transmittals processed. Thus, the total number of transmittals can also be derived. The average number of total transmittals for the largest banks is over 10 million. That number drops considerably for smaller banks with strata 2 and 3 banks only averaging slightly over 27 thousand transmittals. The institutions with unknown assets, largely foreign banks, average just over 1.4 million total transmittals.

Figure 19: Average and median number of funds transmittals processed in 2006

	Banks Stratum 1 (Assets over $1B)	Banks Strata 2 and 3 (Assets $1B and under)	Banks Strata 4 (Assets unknown)	Money Transmitters
Average number of transactions	10,065,825	27,286	1,421,185	23,218,230
Median number of transactions	612,500	1,618	22,000	1,339,467
N	23	8	32	4

Extrapolating from the survey responses to the entire sample for depository institutions provides the following estimates: (1) total number of transmittals from all banks in 2006, (2) total number of transmittals from all banks that were considered reportable in 2006, (3) total number of transmittals under $3,000 that would have otherwise been considered reportable, and (4) total expected number of transmittals in 2010.

Using the average number of total funds transmittals processed in 2006, the total number of transmittals by domestic banks should be on the order of 1 billion*. Calculating this figure for foreign banks is slightly more problematic since there are not much data on how banks are distributed among strata with respect to assets. Using the Stratum 4 average of 1.4 million transactions for all foreign banks yields a figure of 140 million total transactions. However, should Stratum 1averages be more appropriate (10 million transactions) even for half of the foreign bank population, then the number of transmittals would be significantly higher – closer to 570 million total transactions. Thus, the total number of foreign transmittals processed in 2006 is estimated to range from between 140 and 570 million**. **Collectively it is estimated from the data supplied by the banks that domestic and foreign banks conducted approximately 1.1 billion to 1.6 billion transmittals in 2006.**

For domestic transmittals multiplying the average number by strata times the number of institutions in each stratum yields the following: (Stratum 1) 10MM x 102 = 1.02 Billion; (Stratum 2 and 3) 27K x 34 = .9M; (Stratum 4) 1.4 MM x 11 = 15.4 MM.

** For foreign transmittals the upper range is derived by the following: (50% of foreign banks Stratum 1) 10MM x 50 = 500MM; (50% of foreign banks Stratum 4) 1.4MM x 50 = 70MM. The lower range uses 1.4MM x 100.*

With respect to the total number of transactions that are under $3,000 but otherwise reportable, banks in stratum 4 and stratum 1, and money transmitters have the highest average number of these types of transactions. Extrapolating the averages to the overall population yields approximately 90 million transactions domestically that are under $3,000 but otherwise reportable*. For the foreign SWIFT bank population the estimated totals are higher with a range of 120 million to 170 million**. **Collectively, it is estimated that foreign and domestic SWIFT banks conducted between 210 million and 260 million of these types of transactions in 2006.**

For domestic transmittals multiplying the average number by strata times the number of institutions in each stratum yields the following: (Stratum 1) 700K x 102 = 71 MM; (Stratum 2 and 3) 2.3K x 34 = 78K; (Stratum 4) 1.7 MM x 11 = 18.7 MM.

** For foreign transmittals the lower range is derived by the following: (50% of foreign banks Stratum 1) 700K x 50 = 35MM; (50% of foreign banks Stratum 4) 1.7MM x 50 = 85MM. The upper range uses the Stratum 4 (1.7MM) x 100.* **The total number of domestic SWIFT banks transactions in 2006 that could be considered reportable based on averages is approximately 143 million*. For foreign SWIFT banks this estimate is between 81 million and 137 million**.**

For domestic transmittals multiplying the average number by strata times the number of institutions in each stratum yields the following: (Stratum 1) 1.37 MM x 102 = 140 MM; (Stratum 2 and 3) 6.2 K x 34 = .2 MM; (Stratum 4) 258K x 11 = 2.8 MM.

** For foreign transmittals the lower range is derived by the following: (50% of foreign banks Stratum 1) 1.37 MM x 50 = 68.5MM; (50% of foreign banks Stratum 4) 258K x 50 = 12.9 MM. The upper range uses the Stratum 4 (1.37MM) x 100 = 137MM.*

Given the strong relationship between the estimates provided for the number of reportable transactions for 2010 and the number of reportable transactions in 2006, **it is estimated that the total number of reportable transactions for domestic SWIFT banks expected in 2010 is approximately 182 million. For foreign SWIFT banks the expected number of reportable transactions in 2010 is estimated to be between 103 million and 174 million***.**
*** Figures for 2010 are derived from 2006 reported figures times the coefficient from the regression between these two variables 1.273.*

Expected cost to implement reporting requirements

The largest domestic SWIFT banks (e.g. with over $1 billion in assets) estimated an average cost of just under 250 thousand dollars for the implementation of systems for the new requirements and an annual recurring cost of just over 82 thousand dollars. There are also a large proportion of respondents that believe the costs will be quite a bit less, as the median costs for stratum 1 banks are just over 100 thousand for implementation and approximately 35 thousand for annual costs.

The average costs are considerably lower for foreign SWIFT banks. The average implementation costs were estimated to be just over 52 thousand and annual costs estimated at approximately 64 thousand dollars. Average and median costs for those with unknown assets and assets of $1billion or less represent a small sample, but are provided below. Again, median costs are considerably lower among foreign banks with implementation estimated at about 40 thousand and annual costs just over 20 thousand.

Figure 20: Average and median expected costs for implementation of new requirement (one-time costs)

	Domestic Banks Stratum 1 (Assets over $1B)	Domestic Banks Strata 2 and 3 (Assets $1B and under)	Domestic Banks Stratum 4 (Assets unknown)	All Foreign Banks
Average one-time implementation cost estimate	249,787	32,167	153,827	52,466
Median one-time implementation cost estimate	101,380	40,000	123,328	39,840
N	17	3	4	31

Figure 21: Average and median expected annual costs of new requirement (recurring annual costs)

	Domestic Banks Stratum 1 (Assets over $1B)	Domestic Banks Strata 2 and 3 (Assets $1B and under)	Domestic Banks Stratum 4 (Assets unknown)	All Foreign Banks
Average annual cost	82,409	37,833	76,853	63,851
Median annual cost	34,625	50,000	36,914	20,496
N	16	3	5	32

Extrapolating the mean (i.e. average) and median cost estimates for one-time implementation and annual costs over the entire population yields the following figures for total costs to domestic and foreign SWIFT banks to execute the new requirement.

Figure 22: Estimated implementation and annual costs to all U.S. and foreign SWIFT banks

Depository Institution Type	Total Population	Total Implementation Cost (Based on Median)	Total Implementation Cost (Based on Mean)	Total Annual Cost (Based on Median)	Total Annual Cost (Based on Mean)
Domestic Banks (Assets over $1 Billion)	102	10,340,760	25,478,274	3,531,750	8,405,718
Domestic Banks (Assets $1Billion and under)	34	1,360,000	1,093,678	1,255,076	2,613,002
Domestic Banks (Assets unknown)	11	1,356,608	1,692,097	406,054	845,383
Total Domestic SWIFT Banks	147	13,057,368	28,264,049	5,192,880	11,864,103
Total Foreign SWIFT Banks	100	3,984,000	5,246,600	2,049,600	6,385,100

The table on the previous page derives total costs from multiplying the total population for each organization type or strata by the median and mean costs provided by each group. **The total one-time costs to all domestic SWIFT banks for implementing changes for the proposed requirement ranges from $13 million to just over $28 million.** With the median-derived costs being the lower end of the range and the mean-derived cost being the upper range. As would be expected, domestic SWIFT banks with assets over $1billion would account for a majority of this cost as they comprise 69% of the population in numbers and estimate a significantly higher cost than other domestic groups. Estimates show that the domestic banks with assets over $1billion would account for between 79% and 90% of the total one-time implementation costs to all domestic SWIFT banks. **The estimated annual, or recurring costs would be between just over $5 million to just under $12 million based on extrapolating the median and mean annual costs from the data.**

Foreign SWIFT banks are estimated to have significantly lower total costs. Based on estimated costs provided by respondents, **the total one-time costs to all foreign SWIFT banks for implementation would be between just under $4 million to just over $5 million. Annual costs would range from $2 million to approximately $6.4 million.**

The charts below show a breakdown of one-time implementation and annual costs for all depository institutions (i.e. domestic and foreign SWIFT banks). These figures are from open-end responses to expected expenses that were coded (codes shown in Appendix B) for all respondents. Software/development, systems upgrades and programming are estimated to account for nearly half of the implementation costs. Personnel and on-going management are estimated to account for two-thirds of the annual costs.

Figure 23: One-time implementation costs by source   *Figure 24: Annual costs by source*

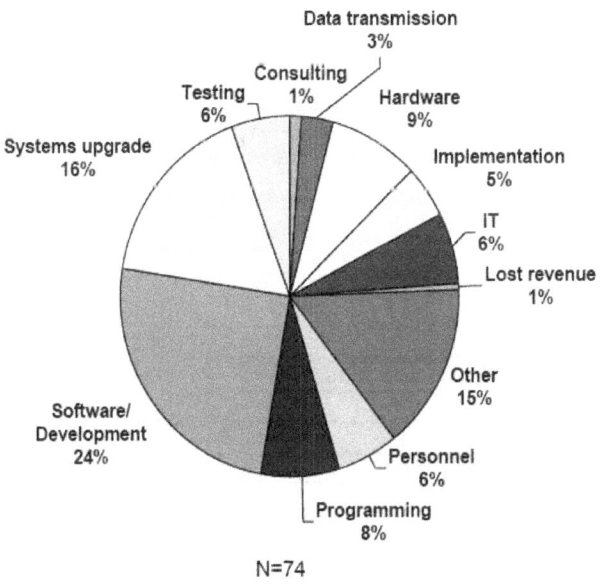

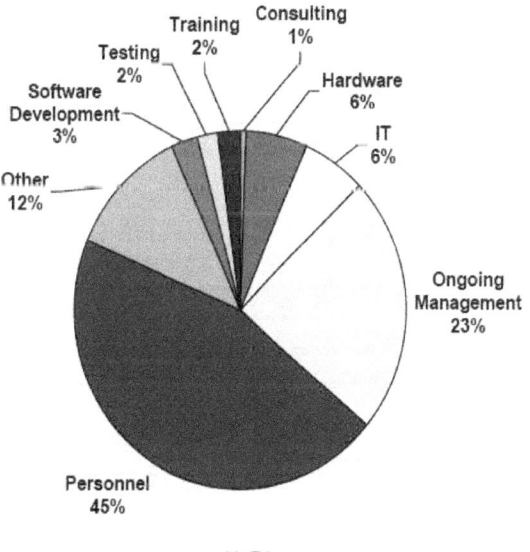

Money Transmitter Costs

Given the small number of money transmitters that responded to the survey, there are very few data points to work with for estimates.

One response was collected from the stratum 1 group (100,000 plus branches). They estimated the implementation cost to be approximately $250,000 and the annual costs to be just over $50,000. **Assuming these costs are representative of the 6 money transmitters of this size, the total implementation costs to this group would be approximate $1.5 million and the total annual costs to the (6) largest money transmitters would be approximately $300 thousand.**

Figure 25: Costs to Stratum 1 – 100,000+ branches

Type of Cost	Pct.of total cost	Total one-time cost
Software/Development	82.8%	250,006
Type of Cost	Pct.of total cost	Total annual cost
Ongoing Management/Transmission	17.2%	51,934

Only one respondent from stratum 2 (1,000 to 100,000 branches) replied and none from stratum 3 replied. The only cost data provided was for implementation, which was $25,000 for personnel. No estimates were given for annual costs. Thus, no data to extrapolate costs to these strata are available from the survey.

Figure 26: Costs to Stratum 2 – 1,000 – 100,000 branches

Type of Cost	Pct.of total cost	Total one-time cost
Personnel/Other	100%	25,000

Very large variations were provided in the three estimates from stratum 4 money transmitters. One respondent gave an estimated annual expense cost of over $1 million, while the two other gave more modest costs of $60,000 and $4,000. Only one of these respondents provided any type of implementation cost ($1,000). Given the large population of this group (8,000+), it would not be possible to extrapolate any reliable total cost to the group from the survey data.

Figure 27: Costs to Stratum 4 – Under 100 branches

Type of Cost	Pct.of total cost	Total one-time cost
Other	20%	1,000
Type of Cost	Pct.of total cost	Total annual cost
IT/Personnel/Other	100%	1,133,548
Personnel	100%	60,000
Personnel	80%	4,000

How the cost of complying with the reporting rule compares to responding to subpoenas

Overall, respondents thought that complying with the potential reporting rule would be more costly than responding to subpoenas. The mean score on a 5-point scale was 3.7 (where 1 means "significantly less costly" and 5 means "significantly more costly.") Across all respondents, 65% thought complying would be slightly or significantly more costly than responding to government subpoenas.

Figure 28: Q3. How the costs of complying with the potential reporting rule would differ from the costs of responding to government subpoenas or other legal demands for the exact same information.

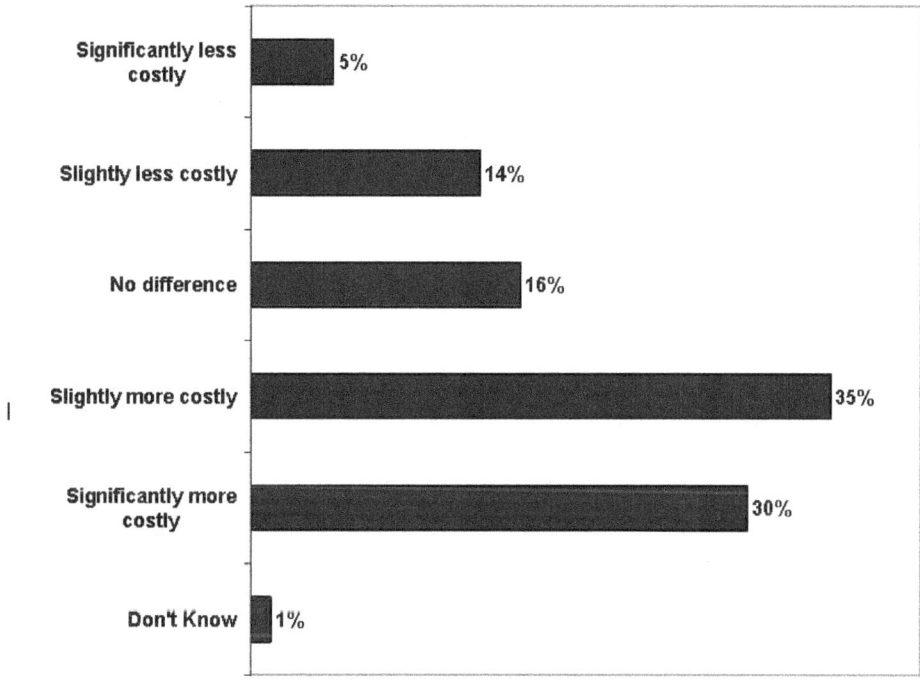

N=81

How the reporting requirement would affect volume, value and quality of transmittals

While they do believe the reporting requirement will affect costs to some degree, for the most part respondents do not believe that the reporting requirements will affect the volume, value or quality of transmittals.

Volume
With respect to volume of transmittals, a majority (59%) thought there would be no change as a result of the requirement. However, 23% thought they would experience a slight or significant decrease and 16% thought there would be a slight or significant increase. The mean score for expected change in volume on a 5-point scale was 2.95 (where 1 means "significant decrease" and 5 means "significant increase.") *Thus, it can be inferred that the expected 27% increase in the number of transmittals from 2006 to 2010 reported by respondents is mostly expected due to an anticipated growth in business or similar factors and not directly from the proposed reporting requirement.*

Value
In considering changes to the value of transmittals a majority (63%) thought there would be no change. As with volume, 23% thought they would experience a slight or significant decrease in value. However, only 12% thought there would be a slight or significant increase. The mean score for expected change in value on a 5-point scale was 2.94 (where 1 means "significant decrease" and 5 means "significant increase.")

Quality
While respondents mostly expected no changes in volume or value of transmittals, the new requirements were expected to have even less of an effect on the quality of transmittals. Over three-quarters of respondents (77%) thought there would be no change in the quality of transmittals. Only 9% thought they would experience a slight or significant decrease and 12% thought there would be a slight or significant increase. The mean score for expected change in value on a 5-point scale was 3.01 (where 1 means "significant decrease" and 5 means "significant increase.")

Figure 29: Q5. Requirements expected effect on volume, value and quality of transmittals

	Volume	Value	Quality
Significant decrease	4%	3%	4%
Slight decrease	19%	20%	5%
No change	59%	63%	77%
Slight increase	11%	6%	9%
Significant increase	5%	6%	3%
Don't Know	3%	3%	4%

Verbatim responses

The following section includes the frequency of coded verbatim comments to all open-ended questions shown by institution type and/or size. Please note, that in those instances where a respondent gave multiple open-ended responses to a question, only the primary or first point was categorized.

Q4. What alternative reporting methods or implementation approaches would reduce the cost to your institution of complying with a potential reporting requirement ? How ?

The most commonly suggested methods for reducing costs to their institution included obtaining information from SWIFT from existing sources, which was mentioned by 19 respondents; less frequent reporting (12 respondents) and an automated system or reporting (9 mentions). Other suggestions with the number of mentions are listed in the table below.

Figure 30: Verbatim comments to: What alternative reporting methods or implementation approaches would reduce the cost to your institution of complying with a potential reporting requirement? How ?

Comment	Domestic SWIFT Banks (Assets over $1 Billion)	Domestic SWIFT Banks (Assets $1 Billion and under)	Domestic SWIFT Banks (Assets unknown)	Foreign SWIFT Banks	Money Transmitters	Total Comments
Obtain information from SWIFT/Existing sources	9	1		8	1	19
Less frequent reporting	2	1	1	8		12
Automated system/Software	4	1	1	2	1	9
Risk-based approach/Higher dollar threshold	1			3		4
Less selective criteria			1			1
Format		1	1			2
Uniform reporting standards					1	1
Use of 314a information gathering mechanism	1					1
Other comments	5		1	1		7
No suggestions	2	1		11		14

In those instances where a respondent gave multiple open-ended responses to a question, only the primary or first point was categorized.

Q5b. Please indicate any other area within your institution that you think maybe effected by the new reporting requirement.

Respondents did not have many comments about the effect that the requirements might have on their institution. Among those effects that were mentioned most were compliance, wire transfers and operations or workload. All comments with number of mentions are listed in the table below.

Figure 31: Verbatim comments to: Please indicate any other area within your institution that you think maybe effected by the new reporting requirement.

Comment	Domestic SWIFT Banks (Assets over $1 Billion)	Domestic SWIFT Banks (Assets $1 Billion and under)	Domestic SWIFT Banks (Assets unknown)	Foreign SWIFT Banks	Money Transmitters	Total Comments
Compliance	3			5		8
Wire transfers	4	1	1			6
Operations/Workload	4	1				5
International/Trade				3		3
Customer Service	1			1		2
Fees		1				1
Other	3		1	1	2	7
Not sure/None	3			2		5

In those instances where a respondent gave multiple open-ended responses to a question, only the primary or first point was categorized.

Q6. Would there be any potential unintended consequences that would adversely affect your institution (e.g., such as an anticipated shift to a competitor or to an informal funds transmittal system or an effect on your institution's business model) associated with such a potential reporting requirement being imposed on all U.S. financial institutions to which the recordkeeping rule applies? Please explain.

For the most part respondents did not think that there would be unintended adverse consequences from the reporting requirement (34 mentions). There was some concern about banks moving wire transfer processing abroad and customers using informal or other funds transmittal systems. Both had 8 mentions. Additional expenses and passthrough to customers was mentioned (5 mentions). Other comments are listed with number of mentions in the table below.

Figure 32: Verbatim comments to: Would there be any potential unintended consequences that would adversely affect your institution (e.g., such as an anticipated shift to a competitor or to an informal funds transmittal system or an effect on your institution's business model) associated with such a potential reporting requirement being imposed on all U.S. financial institutions to which the recordkeeping rule applies? Please explain.

Comment	Domestic SWIFT Banks (Assets over $1 Billion)	Domestic SWIFT Banks (Assets $1 Billion and under)	Domestic SWIFT Banks (Assets unknown)	Foreign SWIFT Banks	Money Transmitters	Total Comments
No effect/No long-term effect	7	2	2	20	3	34
Banks move wire transfer processing abroad	4		1	3		8
Customers using informal/Other funds transmittal systems	1	1		4	2	8
Additional expenses/Passthrough to customers	4	1				5
Operations/Workload			2	2		4
Privacy concerns			2	2		4
Loss of customers	2					2
Additional monitoring	1					1
Slower transmissions	1					1
Wire payment system				1		1
Other				1		1

In those instances where a respondent gave multiple open-ended responses to a question, only the primary or first point was categorized.

Q7. If a potential cross-border funds transmittal reporting requirement was implemented, what would be the value (if any) to your institution of receiving aggregated, industry-wide reports and analysis from FinCEN on cross-border funds transmittal trends, including reports similar to those currently provided for suspicious activity reports?

While the most common response (36 mentions) was that there would be slight or no value from the reports and analysis from the requirement, identifying trends was mentioned as a benefit (19 mentions) as was identifying suspicious activity (7 mentions). Other comments are listed with number of mentions in the table below.

Figure 33: Verbatim comments to: If a potential cross-border funds transmittal reporting requirement was implemented, what would be the value (if any) to your institution of receiving aggregated, industry-wide reports and analysis from FinCEN on cross-border funds transmittal trends, including reports similar to those currently provided for suspicious activity reports?

Comment	Domestic SWIFT Banks (Assets over $1 Billion)	Domestic SWIFT Banks (Assets $1 Billion and under)	Domestic SWIFT Banks (Assets unknown)	Foreign SWIFT Banks	Money Transmitters	Total Comments
Slight/No value	10	1	2	21	2	36
Identifying trends	7	2	2	5	3	19
Identifying suspicious activity	2	2		3		7
Risk assessment	1			3		4
Benchmarking			1	3		4
Significantly valuable				2		2
AML/BSA program	2					2
Monitoring				1		1

In those instances where a respondent gave multiple open-ended responses to a question, only the primary or first point was categorized.

Q8 i. If a potential cross-border funds transmittal reporting regulation was implemented, what types of outreach or guidance from FinCEN regarding its requirements would be most helpful to the financial services industry?

Guidance and outreach most mentioned by respondents include webinars and sessions (12 mentions), technical requirement guidance or targeted guidance (10 mentions), clear instructions (9 mentions). Implementation advice, FAQs and a hotline were also mentioned. Other comments are listed with number of mentions in the table below.

Figure 34: Verbatim comments to: If a potential cross-border funds transmittal reporting regulation was implemented, what types of outreach or guidance from FinCEN regarding its requirements would be most helpful to the financial services industry?

Comment	Domestic SWIFT Banks (Assets over $1 Billion)	Domestic SWIFT Banks (Assets $1 Billion and under)	Domestic SWIFT Banks (Assets unknown)	Foreign SWIFT Banks	Money Transmitters	Total Comments
Webinars/Sessions	3			9		12
Technical requirements guidance/Targeted guidance	7			3		10
Clear instructions		1	1	7		9
Implementation advice	2	1		2		5
FAQs				4	1	5
Hotline		1	2		1	4
Statistics/Standards	2					2
Sufficient time				2		2
Best practices	1					1
Simplify reporting format					1	1
Online database					1	1
Notifications				1		1
Other	5	2	2	6	2	17

In those instances where a respondent gave multiple open-ended responses to a question, only the primary or first point was categorized.

9. How satisfied is your institution with this survey and its ability to provide sufficient information for FinCEN to assess effectively the potential cost to the financial services industry of the potential reporting requirement?

Responses were mostly positive regarding respondents' satisfaction with this survey and the information about the potential reporting requirement being sufficient. The most common comments expressed some degree of satisfaction with the survey process (i.e. satisfied, very/significantly satisfied and slightly satisfied). Others thought considering costs and getting input was a good idea. Very few mentioned that they were not satisfied or less than satisfied.

Figure 35: Verbatim comments to: How satisfied is your institution with this survey and its ability to provide sufficient information for FinCEN to assess effectively the potential cost to the financial services industry of the potential reporting requirement?

Comment	Domestic SWIFT Banks (Assets over $1 Billion)	Domestic SWIFT Banks (Assets $1 Billion and under)	Domestic SWIFT Banks (Assets unknown)	Foreign SWIFT Banks	Money Transmitters	Total Comments
Satisfied	6	2	3	8		19
Very/Significantly satisfied	4			5	2	11
Slightly satisfied	1			7	1	9
Not overly/Not so satisfied	3			2		5
Somewhat/Slightly dissatisfied	1	1		2		4
Somewhat/Reasonably satisfied				2		2
Considering costs/Getting input/Good idea				3		3
Information requested not easily obtained/Difficult to estimate costs	1			1		2
Survey very helpful	1					1
Could be more comprehensive		1				
Want more information about regulation			1			1
Survey is direct				1		1
Deadline too short/Takes too long				1	1	2
Other	1			3		4
No opinion/Cannot answer	5	1	1	2	1	10

In those instances where a respondent gave multiple open-ended responses to a question, only the primary or first point was categorized.

This page intentionally left blank.

APPENDIX A : QUESTIONNAIRE

This page intentionally left blank.

FinCen Banking Act 2007
Page 1

This report is authorized by law [12 U.S.C. §5015]. Your voluntary cooperation in submitting this report is needed to make the results comprehensive, accurate, and timely. FinCEN may not conduct or sponsor, and an organization is not required to respond to, a collection of information unless it displays a currently valid OMB control number. FinCEN regards the individual bank information provided by each respondent as confidential.

Public reporting burden for this collection of information is estimated to average 2 hours per response, including the time to gather and maintain data in the required form, to review the instructions and to complete the information collection. Send comments regarding this burden estimate or any other aspect of this collection of information, including suggestions for reducing this burden, to: Barbra Bishop, Financial Crimes Enforcement Network, Vienna, VA (703) 905-5137 or Barbara.bishop@fincen.gov.

Please include the name and phone number of a person that we can contact should there be questions about your responses.

Thank you for your time and cooperation.

This survey is authorized by the U.S. Office of Management and Budget Control No. 1505- 0191.

Page 2

I. Institution Information

    Type of Institution
    {Choose one}
        ( ) Bank
        ( ) Non-bank financial institution (Money Transmitter)

    Name
    {Enter text answer}

    Contact Name
    {Enter text answer}

    Phone Number
    {Enter text answer}

    Email
    {Enter text answer}

Page 5

B. Potential description of reportable cross-border electronic funds transmittals

For the purpose of responding to this survey, please consider the implications of the following potential regulatory requirement for U.S. financial institutions (banks and certain non-bank financial institutions as defined by 31 C.F.R. § 103.11(n)(1) and (3)) to report certain cross-border electronic transmittals of funds. See glossary of terms for any further necessary clarification of terms.

Potential requirements for banks
1) Report any Society for Worldwide Interbank Financial Telecommunications (SWIFT) MT103 message that meets the following requirements:

a. Reporting U.S. (domestic) bank (a bank that is physically located or doing business within the United States) either directly sends ("last out") the payment order to a foreign bank (a bank that is physically located or doing business outside the United States) or foreign non-bank financial institution (a money transmitter that is physically located or doing business outside the United States) or directly receives ("first in") the payment order from a foreign bank or foreign non-bank financial institution.

b. Record of the payment order already must be retained under the "Funds Transfer Recordkeeping" rule (31 C.F.R § 103.33(e)).
i. Only a single SWIFT MT103 message that meets the requirements of the recordkeeping rule's $3,000 threshold would be reported. Multiple SWIFT MT103 messages involving the same customer that are conducted very closely to one another in time and in the aggregate are valued at $3,000 or more would NOT be reported.

ii. Any transaction exempted from the recordkeeping rule in 31 C.F.R. § 103.33(e)(6) would NOT be reportable.

2) For each reportable message, only the following information (as set forth in the MT103 itself) must be reported:
a. Name and address of the originator
b. Amount of payment order
c. Execution date of the payment order
d. Name of the beneficiary's bank
e. Name, address, account number, or other beneficiary identifier (if available)

3) The domestic (U.S.) bank will batch report this information once every business day to FinCEN using the BSA E-Filing system and using the SWIFT MT103 file format.

Page 6

Potential requirements for nonbank financial institutions (money transmitters)

1) Report any transmittal order that meets the following requirements:

a. Reporting U.S. (domestic) nonbank financial institution (a money transmitter that is physically located or doing business within the United States) either directly sends ("last out") the transmittal order to a foreign bank or nonbank financial institution or directly receives ("first in") the transmittal order from a foreign bank or foreign nonbank financial institution.

b. Record of the transmittal order already must be retained under the "Funds Transfer Recordkeeping" rule (31 C.F.R 103.33(f)).

i. Only a single transmittal order that meets the requirements of the recordkeeping rule's $3,000 threshold would be reported. Multiple orders involving the same customer that are conducted very closely to one another in time and in the aggregate are valued at $3,000 or more would NOT be reported.

ii. Any transaction exempted from the recordkeeping rule in 31 C.F.R. § 103.33(f)(6) would NOT be reportable.

2) For each reportable transmittal order, only the following information (as set forth in the transmittal order itself) must be reported:
a. Name and address of the transmitter
b. Amount of the transmittal order
c. Execution date of transmittal order
d. Name of the recipient's financial institution
e. Name, address, account number, or other recipient identifier (if available)

3) U.S. nonbank financial institutions will batch report this information once every business day to FinCEN using the BSA E-Filing system and a standardized message format established by FinCEN.

Page 7

While going through the survey if you have questions about terminology, please refer back to the glossary of terms on the following 3 pages.

Glossary of Terms

The terms used in the survey generally are defined in 31 C.F.R. § 103.33 and 103.11. The following definitions are provided to assist your institution in better responding to the survey. For a more complete definition of any of the terms used in the survey, please refer to the regulation.

Bank
Each agent, agency, branch or office within the United States or any person doing business as a bank as defined by 31 C.F.R. § 103.11(c).

Beneficiary
The person to be paid by the beneficiary's bank.

Beneficiary's bank
The bank or foreign bank identified in a payment order in which an account of the beneficiary is to be credited pursuant to the order or which otherwise is to make payment to the beneficiary if the order does not provide for payment to a deposit account.

Business day
For purposes of this survey, the term "business day" refers to any day (including weekends or holidays) during which an institution is open for business.

Cross-border transmittal of funds or funds transmittal
A transmittal of funds directly exchanged between a domestic and foreign financial institution. For the purposes of this survey and any potential reporting requirement, only cross-border electronic transmittals of funds are considered.

Deposit account
Transaction accounts, savings accounts, and other time deposits as defined by 31 C.F.R § 103.11(j).

Domestic
Located or doing business within the United States. See 31 C.F.R. § 103.11(k).

Financial institution (institution)
Each agent, agency, branch, or office within the United States of any person doing business, whether or not on a regular basis or as an organized business concern, as a bank (except bank credit card systems) or a money transmitter. See 31 C.F.R. § 103.11(n).

Foreign
Located or doing business outside of the United States or not domestic.

Foreign bank
A bank organized under foreign law, or an agency, branch, or office located outside the United States of a bank. The term does not include an agent, agency, branch or office within the United States of a bank organized under foreign law. See 31 C.F.R. § 103.11(o).

Page 8

Glossary of Terms - Cont.

Foreign financial institution (foreign institution)
A financial institution organized under foreign law, or an agency, branch, or office located outside the United States. The term does not include an agent, agency, branch or office within the United States of a financial institution organized under foreign law.

Funds transfer
The series of transactions, beginning with the originator's payment order, made for the purpose of making payment to the beneficiary of the order. Funds transfers governed by the Electronic Fund Transfer Act of 1978 (Title XX, Pub. L. 95-630, 92 Stat. 3728, 15 U.S.C. 1693, et seq.), as well as any other funds transfers that are made through an automated clearinghouse, an automated teller machine, or a point-of-sale system, are excluded from this definition. See 31 C.F.R § 103.11(q). For the purposes of this survey and any potential reporting requirement, only electronic funds transfers are considered.

Money transmitter
Any person, whether or not licensed or required to be licensed, who engages as a business in accepting currency or funds, or the value of the currency or funds, by any means through a financial agency or institution, a Federal Reserve Bank or other facility of one or more Federal Reserve Banks, the Board of Governors of the Federal Reserve System, or both, or an electronic funds transfer network; or, any other person engaged as a business in the transfer of funds. See 31 C.F.R. § 103.11(uu)(5).

Originator
The sender of the first payment order in a funds transfer.

Originator's bank
The receiving bank to which the payment order of the originator is issued if the originator is not a bank or foreign bank.

Payment order
An instruction of a sender to a receiving bank, transmitted orally, electronically, or in writing, to pay, or to cause to pay, a fixed or determinable amount of money to a beneficiary as defined by 31 C.F.R § 103.11(y).

Person
An individual, a corporation, a partnership, a trust or estate, a joint stock company, an association, a syndicate, joint venture, or other unincorporated institution or group, an Indian Tribe (as that term is defined in the Indian Gaming Regulatory Act codified at 25 U.S.C. 2701-2721 and 18 U.S.C. 1166-68), and all entitles cognizable as legal personalities.

Receiving or recipient's bank
The bank or foreign bank to which the sender's instruction is addressed.

Receiving or recipient's financial institution
The financial institution or foreign financial institution to which the sender's instruction is addressed. The term receiving financial institution includes a receiving bank.

Recipient or receiver
The person to be paid by the recipient's financial institution. The term recipient includes a beneficiary, except where the recipient's financial institution is a financial institution other than a bank.

Page 9

Glossary of Terms - Cont.

Sender
The person giving the instruction to the receiving financial institution.

Transaction
A deposit, withdrawal, transfer between accounts, or payment involving financial institutions.

Transmittal of funds or funds transmittal
The series of transactions, beginning with the originator's payment order, made for the purpose of making payment to the beneficiary of the order, or a series of transactions beginning with the transmitter's transmittal order, made for the purpose of making payment to the recipient of the order. The term "transmittal of funds" includes a funds transfer. Funds transfers governed by the Electronic Fund Transfer Act of 1978 (Title XX, Pub. L. 95-630, 92 Stat. 3728, 15 U.S.C. 1693, et seq.), as well as any other funds transfers that are made through an automated clearinghouse, an automated teller machine, or a point-of-sale system, are excluded from this definition. See 31 C.F.R § 103.11(jj). For the purposes of this survey and any potential reporting requirement, only electronic funds transmittals are considered.

Transmittal order
A payment order or the instruction of a sender to a receiving financial institution, transmitted orally, electronically, or in writing, to pay, or cause another financial institution or foreign financial institution to pay, a fixed or determinable amount of money to a recipient as defined by 31 C.F.R § 103.11(kk).

Transmitter (or transmittor)
The sender of the first transmittal order in a transmittal of funds. The term transmitter includes an originator, except where the transmitter's financial institution is a financial institution or foreign financial institution other than a bank or foreign bank.

Transmitter's financial institution
The receiving financial institution to which the transmittal order of the transmitter is issued if the transmitter is not a financial institution or foreign financial institution or agency, or the transmitter if the transmitter is a financial institution or foreign financial institution or agency. The term transmitter's financial institution includes an originator's bank, except where the originator is a transmitter's financial institution other than a bank or foreign bank.

Page 10

III. Cost to the Financial Services Industry of a Potential Cross-border Electronic Funds Transmittal Reporting Requirement

Please respond in full to the following nine (9) questions and all their associated subparts.

Please refer to the above description of a potential cross-border electronic funds transmittal reporting requirement (see Section IIB on pages 5 and 6) to determine your institution's response. Consider only the electronic funds transfers or transmittals that your institution processes within the United States.

See glossary of terms (pages 7-9) for further clarification of the survey terms.

1. Based upon the description of potentially reportable cross-border electronic funds transfers/transmittals (hereafter "transmittals), would your institution be able to identify the payment or transmittal orders that would need to be reported to FinCEN?
{Choose one}
( ) Yes
( ) No

i. Total number of electronic funds transmittals your institution processed in 2006 that could be considered reportable cross-border electronic funds transmittals (as described in Section II):
{Enter text answer}

a. Percentage of all electronic funds transmittals your institution processed in 2006:
{Enter text answer}

b. Percentage of the total value of all electronic funds transmittals your institution processed in 2006:
{Enter text answer}

Page 11

ii. Total number of electronic funds transmittals your institution processed in 2006 that were valued at less than $3,000 that otherwise would have met all the other requirements to be considered reportable cross-border electronic funds transmittals.
{Enter text answer}

a. Percentage of all electronic funds transmittals your institution processed in 2006:
{Enter text answer}

b. Percentage of the total value of all electronic funds transmittals your institution processed in 2006:
{Enter text answer}

iii. Estimate the number of electronic funds transmittals your institution expects to process in 2010 that could be considered reportable cross-border electronic funds transmittals (as described in Section II):
{Enter text answer}

a. Percentage of all electronic funds transmittals your institution expects to process in 2010:
{Enter text answer}

b. Percentage of the total value of all electronic funds transmittals your institution expects to process in 2010:
{Enter text answer}

2. What would be the total cost (in thousands of U.S. dollars) to your institution to implement the potential reporting requirement described in Section IIB and report the total number of reportable cross-border electronic funds transmittals expected to be processed in 2010?
{Enter text answer}

Please list five (5) major sources of cost to your institution that would be incurred to comply with the potential reporting requirement and indicate the percentage of your estimated total cost for which each accounts. Please also indicate (with an "X") whether it would be a one-time implementation or annual recurring cost.

2.1. Cost in Thousand Dollars
    1. Source of Cost {Enter text answer}
    (2)Type of cost
    {Choose one}
        ( ) Recurring (Annual)
        ( ) Implementation (one-time)

2.2. Cost in Thousand Dollars
    1. Source of Cost {Enter text answer}
    (2)Type of cost
    {Choose one}
        ( ) Recurring (Annual)
        ( ) Implementation (one-time)

2.3. Cost in Thousand Dollars
    1. Source of Cost {Enter text answer}
    (2)Type of cost
    {Choose one}
        ( ) Recurring (Annual)
        ( ) Implementation (one-time)

2.4. Cost in Thousand Dollars
    1. Source of Cost {Enter text answer}
    (2)Type of cost
    {Choose one}
        ( ) Recurring (Annual)
        ( ) Implementation (one-time)

2.5. Cost in Thousand Dollars
    1. Source of Cost {Enter text answer}
    (2)Type of cost
    {Choose one}
        ( ) Recurring (Annual)
        ( ) Implementation (one-time)

Page 13

3. Based upon the following sliding scale, please indicate how the cost of complying with the potential reporting rule would differ from the cost of responding to government subpoenas or other legal demands for the exact same information?

Cost of complying

    Cost of complying
    {Choose one}
        ( ) Significantly less costly
        ( ) Slightly less costly
        ( ) No difference
        ( ) Slightly more costly
        ( ) Significantly more costly

In responding to this question, please consider all the costs associated with your procedures to comply with a government subpoena or other legal demand for similar data. For example, you should consider the cost of extracting the records or data from your systems, data editing, data validation, data formatting, reporting method, and the time commitment of staff to have follow-up discussions with law enforcement and regulators regarding the data.

    4. What alternative reporting methods or implementation approaches would reduce the cost to your institution of complying with a potential reporting requirement? How?
    {Enter answer in paragraph form}

Page 14

5a. Please indicate the effect that you would anticipate that a reporting requirement as described in this survey might have on cross-border electronic funds transmittals involving your institution with respect to the following areas...

Volume
{Choose one}
    ( ) Significant decrease
    ( ) Slight decrease
    ( ) No change
    ( ) Slight increase
    ( ) Significant increase

Value
{Choose one}
    ( ) Significant decrease
    ( ) Slight decrease
    ( ) No change
    ( ) Slight increase
    ( ) Significant increase

Quality or type of payment services provided
{Choose one}
    ( ) Significant decrease
    ( ) Slight decrease
    ( ) No change
    ( ) Slight increase
    ( ) Significant increase

5b. Please indicate any other area within your institution that you think maybe effected by the new reporting requirement.
{Enter answer in paragraph form}

6. Would there be any potential unintended consequences that would adversely affect your institution (e.g., such as an anticipated shift to a competitor or an informal funds transmittal system or an effect on your institution's business model) associated with such a potential reporting requirement being imposed on all U.S. financial institutions to which the recordkeeping rule applies? Please explain.
{Enter answer in paragraph form}

Page 15

7a. How satisfied is your institution with FinCEN's published industry-wide reports and analysis of suspicious activity report filings? Please use a scale from 1 to 10 where 1 means "not at all satisfied" and 10 means "Extremely satisfied."

7b. To what extent do FinCEN's published industry-wide reports and analysis of suspicious activity report filings fall short of or exceed your expectations? Please use a scale from 1 to 10 where 1 means "Fall short of" and 10 means "Exceeds your expectations."

7c. How do FinCEN's published industry-wide reports and analysis of suspicious activity report filing compare to the ideal? Please use a scale from 1 to 10 where 1 means "Not very close to the ideal" and 10 means "Very close to the ideal."

Page 16

7d. If a potential cross-border funds transmittal reporting requirement was implemented, what would be the value (if any) to your institution of receiving aggregated, industry-wide reports and analysis from FinCEN on cross-border funds transmittal trends, including reports similar to those currently provided for suspicious activity reports?
{Enter answer in paragraph form}

Page 17

8a. How satisfied is your institution with the level of outreach and communication FinCEN pursued regarding the potential cross-border electronic funds transmittal reporting rule raised in this survey?
{Enter text answer}

8b. If a potential cross-border funds transmittal reporting regulation was implemented, what types of outreach or guidance from FinCEN regarding its requirements would be most helpful to the financial services industry?
{Enter answer in paragraph form}

9. How satisfied is your institution with this survey and its ability to provide sufficient information for FinCEN to access effectively the potential cost to the financial services industry of the potential reporting requirement?
{Enter text answer}

Page 18

Would your institution be willing to discuss the questions and issues raised in this survey in more detail with FinCEN representatives?
{Choose one}
    ( ) Yes
    ( ) No

Page 19

FinCEN would like to thank you for your time and participation today. Your feedback is greatly appreciated.

Please hit "Finish" to complete the survey.

APPENDIX B : CODES FOR Q2

This page intentionally left blank.

Verbatim responses to Q2 (ii) recoded

Recoded Category	Response
Communications	Communication & Implementation
Consulting	IT consulting and installation
	Legal & consulting
	Outside Consulting
Data Storage Equipment	Data Center/Lines/Set up
	File/Data Archiving
	Mainframe space
	Storage
	Storage and Reporting of Data
	Storage/Data Center/Lines
	System Enhancements
Hardware	Communications Hardware and Transmission Equipment
	Equipment
HR/Labor/Overtime	3 employees
	Administrative staffing costs - reviewing and data preparation
	Annual administrative costs
	Business Operations Annual Overhead
	Extra man-hours to explain to customers about the new requirement
	Extra man-hours to extracts, review and report to FinCEN
	FTE's
	Human Resources
	Increase Staffing
	In-house resources for project management, test, deployment (50 man days x $1100)
	Labor
	Manpower
	Manpower & Maintenance
	Manual staff cost ($50/report)
	Monitoring
	On Site Staff
	Operation staff to work wire rejects
	Overtime
	Personal Cost
	Personnel
	Personnel Costs (salary & bonus)
	Personnel Time
	Personnel to run daily searches and send reports.

	Salary
	Software
	Staff
	Staff Cost
	Staff reporting
	Staff resources
	Staffing
Implementation	Project Implementation
	Cost to implement the appropriate transmission protocol including required security procedures/protocol, to send payment transaction (e.g. transmittals) to FINCEN BSA E-filing system.
Installation	Installation
Installation/Testing	Installation / Testing
IT	Information Tech
	IT Expenses
Loss of revenue	Lost of revenue derived from international wires
	Lost of customers' deposit due to unpleasant experience
Maintenance/Support	Annual Maintenance- Technical support, report management & communications expense
	Equipment Maintenance
	Hardware Maintenance and Miscellaneous
	In-house support for functionality, inquiries, enhancement, etc. (1h/day=31 man days/year x $1100)
	IT Annual Maintenance
	IT ongoing service
	IT/Software Maintenance/Upgrades
	Maintenance
	Maintenance of the system
	Maintenance support
	Ongoing Maintenance
	Ongoing System / IT Support
	Ongoing systems maintenance
	Recurring Transmission Support Costs
	Software Licensing & Maintenance
	Software Maintenance
	System Maintenance
	System support
	Technical Support
	Upkeep/revisions to program
	Yearly hardware and software charges

Monitoring	Labor
	Monitoring
	Production Support, to monitor successful transmission of files daily
Occupancy	Occupancy
Operational	Data Center operational costs (to handle transmission of data to FINCEN).
	Operational
Other	Sundry
Other - Accommodations	Accommodations
Other - Additional	Additional Hardware
Other - Audit & Training	Audit & Training
Other - Cost of funds	Cost of funds
Other - Data Transmission	Data Transmission
Other - Database Management	Database Management
Other - Definition and Design	Definition and Design
Other - Disclosure Requirements	Disclosure Requirements
Other - File/Network Transmission	File/Network Transmission
Other - FinCEN interface	FinCEN interface
Other - Investigations	INVESTIGATIONS
Other - Licensing	License fees
Other - Management	Management
Other - Manual wire uploading	Manual wire uploading into the software
Other - Marketing	Research for process
Other - Ongoing Processing	Ongoing Processing
Other - Production of files, mail costs, etc.	Production of files, mail costs, etc.
Other - Requirements/Review/Analysis	Requirements/Review/Analysis
Other - Supplies	Supplies
Other -Review	Review
Other -Vendor Management	Vendor Management
Programming	Computer Programming
	Initial Programming
	Report programming and setup
Programming Support	Programming Support
Programming/Hardware	Programming /hardware
Project Design	Project Design
Record Keeping	Record Keeping

Reporting	Reporting
	Reporting Modifications
Research	Research
	Marketing effort
Software/Hardware	Software/Hardware
Software/Software Development	Application Development
	Code Development /Testing
	Development
	Development Costs
	Development/Documentation
	IT Batch Process Development
	IT Development
	New software set up and maintenance
	Software Developer work to prepare MT 103 reports.
	Software Development
	Software Maintenance
	Software Upgrade
	Software Upgrade for Reporting
	Staffing
System upgrade	Automation (System)
	Data Storage Equipment
	Enhancement
	IT Enhancements
	New operating system
	System
	System Development
	System development- business requirements, technical design, programming, communications, interface & implementation $500,000 to $750,000
	System programming, program design, coding, testing
	System Purchase
	Systems
Technology	Technology
	Technology costs if information has to be formatted to send.
	Technology development costs to implement the reporting requirement. This includes changes to the Funds Transfer Monitoring System (FTMON). Technology costs include Technology Project Management costs, Business Analysts, and Developers.
	Technology Expenses to produce files

Testing	Coding and Testing
	Quality Assurance and User Testing Costs.
	Testing
	Testing and Quality Assurance
	Testing/Validation
	UAT
	User Acceptance Costs
	User Acceptance Test
Testing/Training	Testing/training
Training	Training

Summary of Survey Responses

The following section summarizes the key points and issues that banks and money transmitters raised in their responses to one of the survey's five (5) open-ended questions and how those responses varied based upon the type and size of responding institution. As many institutions raised multiple points within their survey responses, the total number of responses necessarily exceeds the total number of respondents.

Q4. What alternative reporting methods or implementation approaches would reduce the cost to your institution of complying with a potential reporting requirement? How?

Overall, the vast majority of survey respondents, particularly domestic banks of all sizes, noted that the costs of complying with a cross-border funds transmittal reporting requirement could not be reduced without either further limiting the scope of the requirement or obtaining the information directly from SWIFT. Automation of the reporting process would also generally help reduce costs. A minority of survey respondents, largely foreign banks, however, recommended expanding the reporting requirement to reduce the need for programmatic changes to their software or manual intervention in the reporting process. 74 different respondents offered 83 separate recommendations or comments.

There is no less costly alternative reporting approach *(19 responses)*
More that one out of every five survey respondents noted that the costs to their institutions of complying with a potential cross-border funds transmittal reporting requirement were irreducible, regardless of the reporting method or implementation approach. Foreign banks and money transmitters were the most common type of institution providing this response.

Obtain cross-border funds transmittal information from SWIFT or other central clearinghouse or data repository rather than from the financial institutions directly *(12 responses)*
The single most common suggestion for reducing the cost of compliance with a potential cross-border reporting requirement was for FinCEN to obtain copies of the funds transmittals from SWIFT or another central clearinghouse or data repository rather than the financial institutions. Large (stratum one) and foreign banks, in particular, suggested this approach as a less costly alternative to financial institutions directly reporting cross-border funds transmittal data to FinCEN. Most of these respondents stated that SWIFT, for example, could provide FinCEN a copy of all the reportable cross-border SWIFT MT103 messages at much less cost than the financial institutions. A number of respondents also suggested that such an arrangement should be established with the consent or agreement of the affected financial institutions. A smaller group suggested the data be reported by SWIFT or another central depository or clearinghouse only in response to a specific statutory or regulatory mandate.

Report the cross-border funds transmittal data less frequently (monthly) *(11 responses)*
Only slightly less common a response was the suggestion that the reporting period be less frequent than the daily requirement presented in the survey. A majority of those offering this suggestion advocated that any reporting be monthly in frequency. About an equal number suggested weekly, quarterly, or annual reporting. Foreign banks were most likely to suggest adopting a less frequent reporting regime and most likely to recommend the reporting time period be monthly.

Provide an automated system or software for reporting cross-border data
(10 responses)
Another common response involved the financial institutions' desire for FinCEN to make available to the industry an automated tool or system for reporting cross-border funds transmittal data or at a minimum provide the electronic interface with FinCEN for such automated data reporting. The common point expressed was that the reporting of this data, if required, should not involve any manual intervention. While foreign banks were slightly more likely to make this suggestion, it also was recommended within each category of surveyed institutions.

Enhance the use of current subpoena, 314(a), and SAR filing systems as an alternative to the creation of a new cross-border funds transmittal reporting requirement *(7 responses)*
Respondents believe that an enhanced use of current subpoena, 314(a), and SAR filing systems would be a more effective means to provide law enforcement with information about potential criminal activity than a general reporting requirement for cross-border funds transmittals. For example, several respondents noted that use of the 314(a) process may produce better results for law enforcement and reduce costs for the responding financial institution, particularly if the request is well targeted along specific risk-based criteria. Others generally noted that the current legal process for obtaining access to cross-border funds transmittal information (whether through subpoena, legal demand letter, or national security letter) works well and no new requirement is necessary for law enforcement or FinCEN to obtain this data. As all these systems and processes are already well-established at financial institutions, the additional costs to enhance these efforts would be minimal. These suggestions largely came from the large bank respondents.

Expand the scope of a potential reporting requirement by not including a value or other reporting threshold *(7 total responses)*
Respondents noted that it may be less costly to report the entire cross-border funds transmittal messages than a limited subset of the data contained in the message. Such an approach would improve the efficiency of the reporting requirement and reduce the need for manual intervention to properly identify the reportable transactions. These respondents noted that a more expansive reporting requirement would reduce their programming and other information technology costs compared with a limited cross-border reporting requirement. In fact, a few respondents suggested that it would be less costly if FinCEN received a copy of all funds transmittals, regardless of whether they were cross-border or domestic. Nearly all these responses were from foreign banks.

Reduce the scope of a potential reporting requirement through the application of additional risk-based criteria or a higher dollar threshold *(6 responses)*
Respondents suggested that FinCEN further refine and better target the definition of reportable cross-border funds transmittals. Two respondents suggested a higher value threshold, such as a $10,000 and above limit that would be consistent with the reporting threshold for current currency transactions. Two other respondents noted that better geographic targeting of countries of concern (with or without a more specific value threshold) or other risk-based criteria, such as the lack of a "reasonable connection" between the parties involved in the transaction would limit the number of transactions reported and therefore the reporting financial institution's cost. Another respondent suggested that FinCEN establish a minimum number of transactions for financial institutions to report. Foreign banks were most likely to suggest that FinCEN further refine the scope of any potential cross-border funds transmittal reporting requirement.

Accept cross-border data in the format stored or used by the financial institution (6 total responses)

Respondents generally agreed that FinCEN should be able to accept cross-border data in the format used by the financial institution. In some cases, this also would mean that FinCEN should not expect all required data fields to be included in the reported message format. This is because, even when certain data fields are required to be included in a SWIFT or proprietary message format, that data still is not always included in the funds transmittal. To the extent that FinCEN can identify the specific data fields to be reported within a given format, the respondents believe that would also help reduce their costs of reporting. Any reporting requirement that required a reformatting of the data, however, would increase compliance costs. Only banks suggested this refinement to the potential reporting requirement illustrated in the survey, with responses from every size strata.

Other responses related to limiting the costs of a potential cross-border reporting requirement (5 total responses)

The remaining survey responses noted various cost-related issues that FinCEN should incorporate into any future consideration of a cross-border reporting requirement. For example, respondents noted law enforcement access to cross-border might actually increase the number of government subpoenas or legal demands sent to financial institutions for other customer data and official bank records, thereby increasing overall compliance costs even if the total number of cross-border funds transmittal subpoenas decreased. Others noted that costs would be affected significantly by how FinCEN ultimately implements any reporting requirement. For example, the clarity of a reporting requirement and the implementation timetable would affect financial institutions' cost of implementation. Others emphasized that any reporting requirement should apply equally to all types of institutions, could replace other regulatory obligations of the reporting institutions, or would be overly burdensome for small volume institutions. Most of these responses came from large banks.

Q5b. Please indicate the effect that you would anticipate that a reporting requirement as described in this survey might have on cross-border electronic funds transmittals involving your institution.

Overall, banks and money transmitters expect that a potential cross-border reporting requirement will most affect their internal compliance and audit areas or wire transfer and other operational departments, particularly at large U.S.-chartered banks. Each type of respondent also noted that a cross-border reporting requirement would affect some aspect of their relationship with their customers, including the services being provided.

Effects of a potential cross-border reporting requirement on financial institutions' activities and departments		
Activity or department	**Number of responses**	**Typical institution providing response**
Compliance and audit departments	18	Large domestic banks and foreign banks
Operations and wire transfer department	15	Large domestic banks
Customer service/relationship	7	Large banks
Information technology (IT)	6	Large domestic banks
Bank Secrecy Act (BSA) activities	5	Large banks

International banking/trade finance	5	Foreign banks
Other	5	Large banks
TOTALS	**61**	**Large domestic banks**

Respondents pointed to the need to increase compliance and audits functions related to BSA compliance, and other related controls and procedures, as the most common effect of a reporting requirement on their institution's internal operations. Respondents also stated that some customers may choose to conduct transactions outside of the United States using currencies other than the U.S. dollar or to structure certain of their transactions to avoid the reporting requirement.

Q6. Would there be any unintended consequences that would adversely affect your institution (such as an anticipated shift to a competitor or to an informal funds transmittal system or an effect on your institution's business model) associated with such a potential reporting requirement being imposed on all U.S. financial institutions to which the recordkeeping rule applies? Please explain.

Overall, financial institutions felt that there could be potentially significant harm to their institutions and the U.S. financial system as a result of new regulation to require financial institutions to report certain cross-border funds transmittals. The most important concern raised was the adverse affect that such requirements would have on the competitive position of the reporting institutions in the United States. A significant number or respondents, however, did not expect any unintended consequences to result from the institution of a cross-border reporting requirement. Other responses highlighted the effects such a requirement could have on the efficiency of the U.S. payments system, additional costs of reporting institutions to address customer evasion of the reporting requirement, customers' financial privacy, and the price of funds transmittals.

Cross-border reporting requirements would harm the competitive position of reporting institutions in the United States and the United States as a global financial center (41 responses)

International wire transfer business currently conducted within the United States will move overseas and no longer be conducted using U.S. dollars (15 responses)
A similar number of U.S.-chartered (mostly large banks) and foreign banks operating within the United States stated that customers may transfer their international wire transfer activity and potentially other financial transactions overseas should a cross-border reporting requirement be implemented. Respondents cited the growing competition from offshore clearing systems that would directly benefit from customers shifting their international funds transmittal and other business from the U.S. to another global financial center. Equally important to the respondents was the effect this shift would have on the continued use and strength of the U.S. dollar as an international currency, with the beneficiary being the Euro and other global currencies.

Some respondents also noted that existing U.S. regulatory requirements have already led them to exit certain business lines. These respondents further stated that they would exit the U.S. international wire transfer market or move their operations overseas should a cross-border reporting requirement be adopted, thereby closing U.S. operations and eliminating financial services sector jobs. Finally, respondents stated that customers may not just move their payment activity out of the United States but also move it to countries with much less transparency than the United States.

Reporting requirement could lead to a competitive imbalance between reporting and non-reporting financial institutions (14 responses)
A number of respondents, particularly large U.S.-charted institutions (8 respondents) and foreign banks doing business in the United States (5 respondents), indicated that the imposition of a cross-border reporting requirement could create a competitive imbalance between reporting and non-reporting financial institutions. This imbalance would be reduced, however, to the extent that a potential reporting requirement applied to all financial institutions (bank and nonbank) located or operating within the United States. This competitive imbalance could also exist between U.S. and non-U.S. located institutions due to less stringent legal and regulatory requirements in other countries, unless broader global agreement on common reporting standards and requirements were established.

Reporting institutions will lose customers and revenues to other domestic competitors and funds transmittal systems (12 responses)
Nearly each category of survey respondent indicated that a potential cross-border reporting requirement would lead to a loss of customers to other domestic competitors, particularly informal value transfer systems, or other formal international funds transfer systems, such as credit, debit, or prepaid payment card systems, negotiable instruments, or the automated clearinghouse (ACH).

No unintended consequences expected with a cross-border reporting requirement (32 responses)
The largest individual group of survey responses, by contrast, indicates that many banks and money transmitters do not expect any unintended consequences as a result of implementing a cross-border funds transmittal reporting requirement. Foreign banks were significantly more likely to state (20 out of 32 responses) that they expected no adverse consequences from a reporting requirement, while less than ten U.S.-charted banks offered the same comment.

Cross-border reporting requirements will slow the processing of funds transmittals and reduce the overall efficiency of the U.S. payments system (12 responses)
Six foreign banks and six U.S.-chartered institutions, including four large banks, raised as a concern the potential adverse affect on the efficiency of the U.S. payments system from a potential cross-border reporting requirement. Some respondents indicated that, in part, this slowdown would result from internal efforts to ensure sufficient data quality in their reporting submissions to FinCEN, particularly if required field information was missing. Others noted the recurring costs their operational and compliance areas would incur to prepare, validate, and otherwise process and transmit any reports to FinCEN. A cross-section of respondents indicated that banks would increasingly choose to use SWIFT MT202 cover payments or domestic payment systems and correspondent relationships rather than SWIFT MT103s.

Cross-border reporting requirements raise significant privacy concerns for financial institutions and their customers (5 responses)
Several foreign banks and two domestic banks raised several related concerns about an increasing perception within global financial and commercial markets that the United States payment system does not provide adequate privacy for customers' financial transactions. As a result, payments that otherwise would flow through the United States will increasingly occur in overseas financial

centers and be conducted in currencies other than the U.S. dollar. Finally, these reporting requirements may conflict with the privacy laws and regulations of other countries and open the reporting institution to litigation or governmental action.

Cross-border reporting requirements will increase subpoenas of financial institution data and customer willingness to structure transactions (5 responses)
A handful of banks and one money transmitter indicated that some customers likely would attempt to evade a cross-border reporting requirement by structuring more of the transactions. To identify these new structuring activities, these institutions will need to invest in additional monitoring and analysis capabilities and systems. As a result, these institutions expect to increase their filing of suspicious activity reports and investigation of potential anti-money laundering activities. These institutions also expect to receive an increasing number of subpoenas, either as a result of the increase in SAR filings or AML investigations or because of the substantial additional data available to law enforcement from the cross-border reporting. These additional BSA compliance activities would further increase the costs to these institutions of a cross-border reporting requirement.

Cross-border reporting compliance costs will be passed along to reporting institution customers (3 responses)
Mostly large U.S.-charted banks indicated that they would have to pass along the costs of complying with a cross-border reporting requirement to their customers.

Q7. If a potential cross-border funds transmittal reporting requirement was implemented, what would be the value (if any) to your institution of receiving aggregated, industry-wide reports and analysis from FinCEN on cross-border funds transmittal trends, including reports similar to those currency provided for suspicious activity reports (SARs).

Overall, approximately 52 percent of all survey respondents indicated that some type of industry-wide report and analysis from FinCEN on cross-border funds transmittals would be of measurable or significant value to their institutions. The remaining respondents indicated, however, that such reports would provide little to no measurable value to their institutions. Among those institutions that stated that such reports would be valuable, there were four general purposes to which the information in the reports might be applied: 1) trend analysis and identification, 2) identification and description of suspicious activities, 3) refinement of the institution's existing cross-border funds transmittal BSA program and associated monitoring and risk assessment activities, and 4) benchmarking an institution's business against the rest of the industry. To be truly useful for those purposes, however, most of those institutions indicated that the information included in the reports must be at a more detailed level than is currently provided in FinCEN's SAR activity reviews. Some institutions also noted that such a report would also be more useful if it included feedback from law enforcement and FinCEN on the usefulness of the data, including the number of investigations, arrests, convictions, fines, etc. directly associated with its use.

Value of cross-border funds transmittal reports to financial institutions		
Survey response	Total number of responses*	Institution type most likely to provide this response

		(by percentage of responses)
Slight or no value	37	Foreign banks
Some measurable value	40	Small U.S. banks
Trend analysis	21	Money transmitters
Suspicious activity analysis	9	Small U.S. banks
Refinement of BSA program	8	Foreign banks
Industry benchmarking	4	U.S. banks with unknown assets
* Individual responses may indicate more than one potential use for such a report		

Q8. If a potential cross-border funds transmittal reporting requirement was implemented, what types of outreach or guidance from FinCEN regarding its requirements would be most helpful to the financial services industry.

Survey respondents were very clear that they would require detailed outreach and guidance from FinCEN should a cross-border reporting requirement be implemented. In addition to written guidance, the industry requested that FinCEN also conduct special outreach or training events and make available technical and other experts via a telephone hotline. The respondents also noted that implementing any reporting requirements would require substantial lead-in time to create and test the reporting systems. This process could take as much as 12 to 18 months for some institutions. Finally, some respondents noted other more general concerns and issues that should be addressed within any reporting requirement, including receiving ongoing feedback from law enforcement and FinCEN on the value of the reported data, possible exemption of small volume institutions from the reporting requirement, and safe harbor provisions to address concerns involving the privacy of their customers' financial information.

Provide detailed technical requirements and implementation guidance, reporting definitions, and other related compliance expectations or advice (36 responses)
There was a clear consensus among survey respondents that FinCEN would need to provide fairly detailed technical and implementation guidance to facilitate those institutions' compliance with a potential cross-border reporting requirement. This would include providing a clear and detailed explanation of the reporting requirement and detailed technical specifications and file formats that would be necessary for institutions to construct the systems they may need to collect and transmit the data to FinCEN. Finally, FinCEN should provide any guidance regarding red flags or other important risk factors that also would help the reporting institutions appropriately monitor these transactions.

Conduct webinars, seminars, and other training sessions that address both general and technical issues associated with the reporting requirement (14 responses)
In addition to clear and detailed guidance and implementation requirements, large banks and foreign banks indicated that there would be substantial value in conducting additional outreach to the industry. This would include holding webinars, seminars, and other

training or informational sessions that would address both general and technical issues associated with a potential reporting requirement.

Publish frequently asked questions (FAQs) and answers
(12 responses)
Most types of banks as well as at least one money transmitter noted that the publication of frequently asked questions and answers would provide helpful guidance to the industry. Some respondents also asked that FinCEN provide some form of interactive web-based system to allow reporting institutions to submit more specific questions and quickly receive an e-mail or other response.

Establish a hotline for general and technical reporting questions (8 responses)
All types of respondents were supportive of establishing a special hotline to address both general and technical questions associated with a potential reporting requirement. Financial institutions would expect that the employees of that hotline would be knowledgeable of both the general and specific technical requirements of the reporting requirement and be able to provide advice either during the call or with minimal intervening delays.

Provide sufficient implementation lead time and testing opportunities before requiring compliance with the reporting requirement (8 responses)
Large banks, foreign banks, and money transmitters noted that the industry would benefit from a phased-in implementation and a testing period before institutions begin reporting the data. For any reporting requirement there would need to be time allotted for reporting institutions to test their capability to transmit data successfully to FinCEN. The recommended amount of time that institutions would require to be able to implement a reporting program would likely vary depending upon the exact reporting requirement. Suggestions ranged from and estimated 90 days to at least 12 to 18 months. Finally, at least one institution noted that the reporting schedule should not conflict with other major regulatory reporting requirements.

Provide periodic feedback to industry on reporting issues and the use and value of the data to law enforcement and FinCEN (4 responses)
A handful of institutions recommended that FinCEN continue its outreach on a potential reporting requirement beyond the initial implementation period. Some respondents requested that FinCEN provide them periodic feedback on any updates related to the implementation of the reporting requirement and related technical issues. Most requested that law enforcement and FinCEN provide them with some feedback regarding how the reported data was actually being used and its realized value to any ongoing or completed investigative or regulatory efforts.

Exempt institutions with minimal cross-border electronic funds transmittal volumes from the reporting requirement (3 responses)
A few respondents noted that any reporting requirement should be refined so that entities with minimal cross-border electronic funds transmittal volumes would be exempted from any reporting requirement.

Address privacy concerns of financial institutions and their customers (2 responses)
Two institutions also raised concerns regarding the protection of the privacy of their customers' financial information. In particular, they asked that FinCEN establish "safe harbor" provisions for reporting financial institutions to avoid any conflict with existing financial privacy laws and regulations.

Appendix D: Acronyms

BSA	Bank Secrecy Act
BSAAG	Bank Secrecy Act Advisory Group
CBFT	Cross-Border Funds Transfer
CBP	U.S. Customs and Border Protection Agency
CI	Criminal Investigation
CID	Criminal Investigation Command
CTR	Currency Transaction Report
DEA	Drug Enforcement Administration
DI	Depository Institution
ETL	Extract, Transform, and Load
FBI	Federal Bureau of Investigation
FCPA	Foreign Corrupt Practices Act
FinCEN	Financial Crimes Enforcement Network
FIU	Foreign Investigative Unit
ICE	Bureau of Immigration and Customs Enforcement
IT	Information Technology
MOU	Memorandum of Understanding
MSB	Money Services Business
MV&S	Modernization Vision and Strategy
OFAC	Office of Foreign Assets Control
OIG	Office of Inspector General
ROM	Rough Order of Magnitude
SAR	Suspicious Activity Report
SB/SE	Small Business/Self Employed
SDLC	Systems Development Life Cycle
SEC	Securities and Exchange Commission
SWIFT	Society for Worldwide Interbank Financial Telecommunications
TTU	Trade Transparency Unit